Hans-Christian Hagman

European Crisis Management and Defence: The Search for Capabilities

Routledge
Taylor & Francis Group

LONDON AND NEW YORK

Adelphi Paper 353

First published December 2002 by **Oxford University Press for**
The International Institute for Strategic Studies
Arundel House, 13–15 Arundel Street, Temple Place, London WC2R 3DX

This reprint published by Routledge
2 Park Square, Milton Park, Abingdon, Oxon, OX14 4RN
For the International Institute for Strategic Studies
Arundel House, 13-15 Arundel Street, Temple Place, London, WC2R 3DX
www.iiss.org

Simultaneously published in the USA and Canada
By Routledge
711 Third Avenue, New York, NY 10017,USA

First issued in hardback 2017

Routledge is an imprint of the Taylor & Francis Group, an informa business

Director John Chipman
Editor Mats R. Berdal
Assistant Editor Matthew Foley

British Library Cataloguing in Publication Data
Data available

Library of Congress Cataloguing in Publication Data

ISBN 13: 978-0-1985-2799-2 (pbk)
ISBN 13: 978-1-1384-6670-8 (hbk)

Contents

Glossary

ABCCC	Airborne Battlefield Command and Control Centre
ALSL	Alternative Landing Ship Logistics
ARRC	Allied Command Europe Rapid Reaction Corps (NATO)
AWACS	Airborne Warning and Control System
C³	Command, Control and Communications
CBRNE	Chemical, Biological, Radiological, Nuclear and Enhanced high explosive
CDM	Capabilities Development Mechanism (EU)
CFSP	Common Foreign and Security Policy (EU)
CJTF	Combined Joint Task Force (NATO)
CONOPS	Concepts of Operations
COREPER	Committee of Permanent Representatives (EU)
COP	Contingency Operations Plans
DoD	Department of Defense (US)
DCI	Defence Capabilities Initiative (NATO)
DSACEUR	Deputy Supreme Allied Commander Europe (NATO)
EC	European Community
ECAP	European Capabilities Action Plan (EU)
ESDI	European Security and Defence Identity
ESDP	European Security and Defence Policy (EU)
EMU	European Monetary Union
EU	European Union
EUROCORPS	European Corps

EUROMARFOR	European Maritime Force
FAWEU	Forces Answerable to Western European Union
GDP	Gross Domestic Product
GPS	Global Positioning System
HFC	Helsinki Force Catalogue (EU)
HHC	Helsinki Headline Catalogue (EU)
HPC	Helsinki Progress Catalogue (EU)
HTF	Helsinki Headline Goal Task Force (EU)
HQ	Headquarters
ICC	International Criminal Court
ICRC	International Committee of the Red Cross
IFOR	Implementation Force (NATO)
IMF	International Monetary Fund
J-STARS	Joint-Surveillance Target Attack Radar System
JV	Joint Vision (US)
KFOR	Kosovo Force (NATO)
LPD	Landing Platform Dock
NAC	North Atlantic Council (NATO)
NATO	North Atlantic Treaty Organisation
NBC	Nuclear Biological and Chemical
NGO	Non-Government Organisation
NRF	NATO Response Force
OCCAR	Organisation Conjointe de Coopération en matière d'Armement
OPLAN	Operations Plan
OSCE	Organisation of Security and Cooperation in Europe
PfP	Partnership for Peace (NATO)
RMA	Revolution in Military Affairs
SACEUR	Supreme Allied Commander Europe (NATO)
SACLANT	Supreme Allied Commander Atlantic (NATO)
SAS	Special Air Service (UK)
SEAD	Suppression of Enemy Air Defence
SFOR	Stabilisation Force (NATO)
SG/HR	Secretary-General of the Council of the EU/High Representative for the CFSP
SHAPE	Supreme Headquarters Allied Powers Europe (NATO)

SITCEN	Joint Situation Centre (EU)
UAV	Unmanned Aerial Vehicle
UN	United Nations
UNPROFOR	UN Protection Force
WEAG	Western European Armaments Group
WEU	Western European Union

Introduction

For decades, the countries of Western Europe depended on US protection for their security. Today, the European Union (EU) has become a net exporter of security. The question that now confronts European governments and institutions is how much *more* security they should be producing and projecting, and with what means. Much of the debate over European and transatlantic capabilities has focused on institutional labels, defence expenditures, costly procurement projects and comparisons between European military potential and US military power. However, the real question is how much more individual European governments can and wish to do in the security field, and which new formulas can produce greater output. The debate about capabilities is really a debate about the extent of Europe's ambition for an active, responsible role in international security, and whether Europe's societies deem acceptable the risks and sacrifices that this would entail.

The outcome of this debate will be shaped by wider changes in the old paradigms of security. The boundaries between military and civilian security and between external and internal security have become more fluid, and economic and social inter-dependence, both within Europe and between Europe and the rest of the world, has increased. As the US focuses increasingly on homeland defence, counter-terrorism and crisis regions beyond Europe, Europe itself must be prepared to take more responsibility for its own security. That governments and publics on both sides of the Atlantic have different perceptions of the shape of the threat and the meaning of multinational cooperation only adds to this complexity.

The EU's approach to security has been based on the conviction that military means are just one element of an effective, sustainable security policy, and usually not the most important one. While this may in part reflect perceptions distorted by the specific experience of the East–West confrontation in Europe, it also corresponds with the belief that not every problem has a military solution. This leads to a broader understanding of capabilities: the ability to 'manage' crises, or better still prevent them. Europe's advantage is seen as lying in precisely this cocktail of security-related measures and activities.

The EU's priorities and modes of operation will never be the same as those in the US, in NATO or in US-dominated warfighting coalitions. It is not sufficient to compare European and US defence spending or military assets. European capabilities must be judged over the whole spectrum of security-projection measures, and in relation to accepted political goals. Hoping for significantly increased defence budgets would be unrealistic in the current political climate in most European countries. The corset of macro-economic performance imposed by European Monetary Union (EMU), together with high unemployment, ageing populations and growing healthcare costs, leaves little room for defence-related growth. Besides, structural changes are often slow and politically painful, and rarely produce rapid savings. For added capabilities, coordination and cooperation need to increase in all areas relevant to security, including diplomacy, the military, the police, civil emergency protection, post-conflict reconstruction, international trade and economic measures. The issue is how to get more out, with limited resources.

This paper answers this question by looking at both the military and the civilian components of conflict prevention and crisis management. It argues that the main opportunities for increasing European capabilities lie in expanding national and functional coordination within Europe; enhancing the EU's strategic decision-making; developing the spectrum of European non-military and military capabilities; and establishing rational and pragmatic cooperation mechanisms between the EU and

NATO, and between the EU and the US. The paper has four objectives:

- to assess the substance of military and civilian capability initiatives by both NATO and the EU;
- to analyse the development of EU instruments and capabilities, and their operational consequences;
- to assess the prospects for strategic partnership between the EU and the US, and the role of European capabilities therein; and
- to identify the major challenges and opportunities in increasing European capabilities for conflict prevention and the management of international crises.

The first chapter describes and assesses initiatives to strengthen European capabilities up to and including NATO's Prague Summit in November 2002.[1] The second chapter discusses likely short-term developments, including a detailed scrutiny of the EU's crisis-management tools. The next chapter analyses US reactions to the European Security and Defence Policy (ESDP) and transatlantic burden-sharing after 11 September, and looks at options for a new strategic partnership between the EU and the US. Chapter four deals with the long-term operational and strategic limitations that Europe faces, and the final chapter enumerates five areas where European capabilities could be significantly increased.

In its use of key terms, this paper assumes that crisis-management *capabilities* are more than just an assembly or catalogue of *assets*, be they mechanised infantry battalions, mine-sweepers, strike aircraft, civilian rescue helicopters or police officers. First, there are both military and civilian crisis-management capabilities. Second, in addition to field capabilities, national and institutional planning and politico-military coordination and decision-making capabilities must be taken into account. Third, just because a state or organisation has an asset, this does not mean that it has a capability: a capability exists only when the asset is relevant to the task at hand.[2] An asset must have the relevant level of training, equipment, deployability, sustainability and effectiveness for it to be a capability in a particular operation or function. This also means that the term 'capability' is relative; there is no exact or comparative qualitative dimension.

Defining *crisis management* and *conflict prevention* – and thus the ESDP's sphere of application – is particularly difficult since individual EU member states have their own definitions and ambitions. Indeed, even within national governments different ministries have different agendas and definitions. The pragmatic solution, adopted in this paper, has been to not define these terms at all, thus granting a degree of constructive ambiguity. Instead, this paper distinguishes between three broad categories: 'military crisis management', 'civilian crisis management' and 'conflict prevention'.[3]

Of course, all of these categories are of secondary importance next to vital interests, including collective and common security commitments and the territorial defence.[4] However, even within the EU and NATO, one member state's crisis management can easily be another's safeguarding of vital interests. Consequently, commitments to crisis management and conflict prevention, and the underlying perceptions of risk, morale, values and acceptable costs, have considerable implications for core aspects of defence and alliance strength in the pursuit of international peace and security.

Chapter 1

Capability Initiatives

NATO's Defence Capabilities Initiative

NATO's Defence Capabilities Initiative (DCI) is often perceived as a reaction to the European deficiencies highlighted by *Operation Allied Force* in Kosovo in 1999. [1] According to the US Department of Defense (DoD), the European allies were particularly weak in precision strike, mobility and command and control and communications (C^3), and lacked sufficient strategic lift and aircraft for intelligence, surveillance and reconnaissance (European nations did, however, have sufficient tactical and operational airlift). [2] Poor doctrinal and technical interoperability among the allies were seen as further challenges. [3]

In fact, the DCI began as a US initiative in June 1998, designed to address the growing technological gap between the US and its NATO allies, the strategic de-coupling of Europe and the US and declining European defence budgets and procurement. Increased European defence spending and off-the-shelf procurement of capabilities were seen as the solution. By late 2002 and the NATO Summit in Prague, however, little had changed in US and European perceptions of capabilities.

The DCI was seen in the US as a blueprint for NATO's response to the US-led Revolution in Military Affairs (RMA) and Joint Vision (JV) doctrines. [4] However, faced with obvious European weaknesses during the Kosovo campaign, the DCI was transformed into NATO policy just ahead of the Washington Summit, and was adopted with little debate. [5] Significantly, the goals were not the result of a comprehensive NATO assessment, nor were they linked to any specific scenarios.[6] With hindsight, the DCI was narrowly focused on military capabilities and towards conventional military crisis management. Nevertheless, the DCI did add momentum to European defence restructuring, and its effects will be felt throughout the decade.

The DCI identified 58 vital upgrade goals in deployability and mobility, sustainability and logistics, effective engagement, the survivability of forces and infrastructure and command-and-control and information systems.[7] Several involved the military use of commercial sea and airlift, the sharing or pooling of transport assets, establishing multinational logistic units and expanding logistics and support forces. Other goals included acquiring precision-guided munitions, all-weather weapon systems, unmanned aerial vehicles (UAVs), stealth aircraft, cruise missiles and non-lethal weapons. Nuclear, biological and chemical (NBC) protection and C^3 were also covered, as were 'softer' areas to do with concepts, policies and doctrines. Several goals related to battlefield ground surveillance (such as Joint-STARS) and theatre- and ballistic-missile defence.[8] The DCI was noticeably similar to the 'wish-lists' of the US and the Western European Union (WEU), and the French and British after-action reports on Kosovo.

Of the 58 goals, a number were seen as 'low-hanging fruits' – delivering additional capabilities reasonably quickly, and without great cost. Most coordination, cooperation and training objectives fell into this category. The DCI was also seen as a mechanism for increasing interoperability in peace-support operations. A majority of the goals were applicable to NATO partners, and were channelled to the Partnership for Peace (PfP) planning and review process.[9]

Different perceptions of the DCI

Within the alliance, national interpretations of the DCI varied widely. In general, most Eastern European NATO members saw it as a long-term project to be dealt with after they had adapted their own armed forces, a process expected to take ten years or more. Thus, the DCI was seen as geared mostly towards the UK, France and Germany, because most of its elements are expensive, involve advanced technology or take for granted a certain degree of interoperability. Smaller NATO countries welcomed the DCI, but claimed that there was little prospect of them contributing to its large, high-tech projects. France and the UK seemed to interpret the DCI as a confirmation of their own defence-restructuring efforts and as support for some of their pet national projects; the big gain for Europe, they argued, would be if Germany transformed its armed forces in line with DCI goals. Germany took a selective approach to the DCI, stating that only three elements were of interest: strategic lift, command and control and intelligence. Much could be done through increased interoperability, joint doctrines and multinational exercises, and not everything had to be high-tech. In both France and Germany, there was a widespread perception that the DCI was a US shopping list, not least since the only way to quickly acquire new and advanced combat systems was to buy them off the shelf, and that essentially meant buying American.

The US has seen the DCI as a way of getting its allies to 'field a 21st century force'.[10] The problem is that the US and Europe have different perceptions of what such a force should be. For the US, there is a direct parallel between the DCI and its transformational JV 2010 and 2020 ('net-centric warfare') doctrine. The two are part of a common US understanding of the kind of capabilities 're-quired to address the future security environment as seen by the US and NATO'.[11] Although many of the buzzwords from JV 2010 have found their way into the UK's Strategic Defence Review, NATO's Strategic Concept, allied communiqués and the DCI, European willingness to sign up should not be taken for granted.[12]

It would be wishful thinking to believe that all NATO allies agree with the interpretations of the RMA prevalent in the US debate, and much less with a US-led RMA for the alliance. While there is recognition of the need for interoperability with US forces and a growing realisation that technological advances ought to be better exploited for European defence and security, few if any European states have indicated that their own acquisition priorities match those of the US.[13] Furthermore, not all Europeans are yet prepared to accept US-designed concepts for future joint warfare or the US military transformation model.[14] Although these transformation concepts contain valuable components and guiding ideas, for the majority of European defence forces, with a different baseline, different missions and different priorities, the US vision in its entirety lies far over the horizon.

Regardless of the vocal US agenda and the DCI's preoccupation with high technology, its emphasis on interoperable, mobile and effective military capabilities is relevant in most types of international coalition warfare, whatever its nature. Several of the DCI goals – strategic airlift, for example – have less to do with NATO missions in the Euro-Atlantic area or with net-centric warfare visions than with land-based coalition warfare of the kind seen in Iraq in 1991 and in Afghanistan in 2001, and the kind which will characterise future large-scale US-led war-fighting coalitions. Where such DCI goals match EU scenarios and ambitions, the prospects for implementation are probably the best. However, the DCI has enjoyed only limited progress, at least in relation to US objectives. From its launch in 1999, few in NATO's International Staff in Brussels or at the Supreme Headquarters Allied Powers Europe (SHAPE) have been optimistic about the process. The DCI has made little if any difference to the development of European military capabilities.

The WEU audit of assets

In late 1999, European states finalised an audit of the assets and capabilities available for Petersberg tasks.[15] The audit was based on the Forces Answerable to WEU (FAWEU – a catalogue of national forces potentially available for WEU operations), and those committed to the NATO/PfP planning and review process. Although much of the terminology was the same, the audit differed from the DCI in that it focused more on what Europe would need for autonomous operations.

Although the WEU had the necessary forces in terms of numbers to conduct military operations across the Petersberg spectrum, the audit identified a number of capability gaps and weaknesses.[16] 'Severe gaps' were found in airborne C^3, suppressive electronic warfare, combat search and rescue, stealth technology and precision-strike capabilities. The audit concluded that European forces were 'very weak' in military strategic heavy lift, and relied on civilian assets in this area. Capabilities were 'very limited' in intelligence provision at strategic political and military levels, and in deployable secure tactical communications in theatre, air mobility, psychological warfare, deployable combined joint headquarters, deployable combined air operations centres and electronic/signals intelligence. There was also a serious shortfall in the capabilities required for evacuation operations. The audit pointed out that European forces depended on roads for their ground mobility, and that air mobility (helicopters and tactical air lift) was lacking. Although few states reported on civilian assets, the audit concluded that civil–military coordination was also unsatisfactory. Reconstruction and administrative capabilities were weak, and only one country claimed to be able to provide full assistance to a population affected by an NBC attack. Surprisingly, the audit concluded that interoperability, readiness and sustainability were acceptable – a point which questions its credibility given that these remain huge challenges.

In 'realistic' quantitative terms, the audit counted 66 infantry battalions, 18 armoured regiments, two special-forces battalions and four field hospitals.[17] Maritime forces included three aircraft carriers, ten amphibious ships, 75 destroyers and frigates, 59 mine-countermeasures craft, 34 submarines and 62 sealift and support ships. Ship-based air power was deemed sufficient for self-defence, but extremely limited in any strike or area air-defence capacity. In the air, European forces could muster some 152 air-defence fighters, 137 attack aircraft, 144 light-to-medium transport aircraft (C-130s and smaller), 126 small-to-medium lift helicopters, 24 reconnaissance aircraft, 26 air-to-air refuelling aircraft and seven airborne early-warning (AWACS) aircraft. Only one mobile combined air operations centre was committed. While the capability of this asset would initially be limited, it would increase to a level of 600 sorties a day after three months in theatre.

These assets were compared with the 1996–97 WEU Illustrative Profiles/scenarios, drawn up by the WEU and elaborated and developed by the NATO Combined Joint Planning Staff. For the high-end Separation of Parties scenario, involving two divisions (with equivalent air and maritime forces) in a 12-month operation 6,000 km from Brussels, it was concluded that Europe had sufficient land forces, but lacked air assets for strategic lift, suppression of enemy air defence (SEAD) and electronic warfare. For the conflict-prevention scenario (involving a brigade and equivalent air and maritime components, for less than a year, up to 3,500 km away) Europe had all the assets and capabilities required. In the lower-end scenarios, including humanitarian aid and assistance and evacuation operations, European forces could meet almost all of the requirements. In short, in 1999 Europe had the capabilities to manage a small, high-intensity operation, and any lower-intensity conventional military operations. European forces were not capable of larger, complex and/or distant land operations like KFOR, or major air operations like *Allied Force.*

The audit was solely a quantitative exercise based on conventional military forces earmarked for the FAWEU, or identified in NATO's planning processes. Qualitative issues – whether forces were available, deployable, sustainable and interoperable – were not assessed. A majority of declared forces were already double- or triple-hatted or more, and a significant proportion were deployed in peace-support operations. For WEU operations, many assets would have had to be taken out of NATO reaction forces. WEU military staff complained that much of the national data were superficial, and information provided by some states was clearly unrealistic. Unconventional capabilities beyond the traditional Petersberg spectrum (for example defence against chemical, biological, radiological, nuclear and enhanced high explosive (CBRNE) weapons or counter-terrorism) were generally not included in the audit.

The audit was generally critical and realistic in its assessments of Europe's conventional military capabilities. Both WEU military staff and the nations reporting their assets knew that the findings would not be binding, nor would they form the basis for any operational planning within the WEU. The audit also appeared to have been less influenced by national defence-industrial politics than the DCI. By applying the WEU label, which was seen by NATO and the US as relatively harmless, the EU could also use the audit as a springboard towards the Headline Goal, which was agreed at Helsinki in December 1999.

The Headline Goal and the Helsinki Catalogues

The Headline Goal added the first real substance to the European Security and Defence Policy (ESDP).[18] Under the Goal, by 2003 EU member states committed themselves to being able to deploy and sustain forces capable of the full range of Petersberg tasks as set out in the Amsterdam Treaty, including the most demanding, in operations up to corps level (up to 15 brigades or 50,000–60,000 personnel). These forces should be militarily self-sustaining, with the necessary command, control and intelligence capabilities, logistics, other combat-support services and air and naval elements. Member states should be able to deploy in full at this level within 60 days, and to provide smaller rapid-response elements more quickly than this. They must be able to sustain such a deployment for at least one year.[19] The following year, in November 2000, the EU Capabilities Commitment Conference resulted in the Helsinki Force Catalogue (HFC), which constituted the current sum of national commitments. In addition, the Helsinki Headline Catalogue (HHC) represented an assessment of what the EU would need to fulfil the scenarios developed from the Headline Goal. In effect, the HFC and the HHC reflected what EU member states wished to commit to the Headline Goal in 2003, and what capabilities they wanted to create.

At the Cologne Summit in June 1999, EU members agreed that action would be taken 'without prejudice to actions by NATO'.[20] At Helsinki, the phrase 'where NATO as a whole is not engaged' replaced this formula.[21] This wording guarantees the EU full freedom to act autonomously. In EU operations that can be conducted without recourse to NATO assets, the EU is not dependent on NATO consensus, although US and NATO support would be a bonus. The single institutional framework and decision-making autonomy of the EU in EU-only operations is considered non-negotiable. As in any other organisation, the members are sovereign in deciding if, when and with whom they are prepared to cooperate. This includes inviting non-members to participate in EU operations.[22]

The HFC included only a fraction of the EU's 1.8 million soldiers, 160 destroyers and frigates, 75 tactical submarines and 3,300-plus combat aircraft in 2000.[23] The majority of EU member states committed just about all the interoperable capabilities they had, and these states would be hard-pressed to fulfil their commitments. Nevertheless, what has been committed to the Headline Goal represents the elements of a major fighting force, albeit a rather traditional one. The EU Military Staff initially concluded that member states had committed more than enough HQs, combat brigades, combat aircraft and manpower, but not always the right kind of units. The flaws lay in in-theatre transport, AWACS, air-to-air refuelling, SEAD and electronic warfare, plus strategic airlift and sealift. Psychological-operations battalions, cruise missiles, airborne battlefield command and control, UAVs, airborne signals and electronic intelligence and satellite intelligence elements were also lacking.[24] In 2002, Europe did not own a single military wide-body or long-range strategic transport capable of lifting a main battle tank or transporting the bulky *Patriot* missile system. In addition, the quality and/or availability of some of the committed HQs (five operational HQs and four Force HQs) are questionable.

Most force contributions were double-hatted, and had already been offered to UN standby forces, FAWEU, NATO rapid-reaction forces and multinational constellations such as EUROFOR and EUROCORPS. Only a handful of countries committed new or more capable forces to the EU. Almost all countries put severe restrictions on their forces; the majority of supporting units were limited to supporting national contributions, and would only be used to support European allies if paid for their services. As for commitments by non-EU allied and EU candidates, Turkey limited itself to what had previously been listed in the FAWEU, while Norway offered a new contribution to non-NATO European operations of 3,500 soldiers – a significant number, given the country's size and its location in relation to most areas of European crisis management.

Although essentially symbolic, the Europeans offered more forces to the HFC at the Capabilities Commitment Conference than they had assigned to NATO. Greece and Belgium offered a whole brigade to the HFC and only one battalion to NATO-sustained operations. The Netherlands provided one brigade to the EU and two battalions for NATO, and both the Netherlands and Belgium offered considerably more ships to the Headline Goal. The UK, Germany and Turkey provided more than twice as many combat aircraft to the EU as they did to NATO. Although there is a difference between NATO forces allocated to non-Article 5 missions (which in part correlate with NATO rapid-reaction forces) and the Headline Goal, the US took this as a further warning that the EU may increasingly be taken more seriously than NATO. As was the case for assets announced to the WEU Audit, many Headline Goal commitments would have to be taken out of NATO reaction forces for EU use – which would challenge NATO's traditional 'right' to a 'first pick'.

In June 2001, the gap between the HHC – the capabilities deemed necessary – and the HFC – the forces actually committed – was assessed in the first version of the Helsinki Progress Catalogue (HPC). In greater detail than even the WEU Audit, the HPC identified what further capabilities were needed from EU member states, and added some 'new' capability gaps, such as theatre-missile defence, which cannot easily be categorised as part of the traditional Petersberg spectrum.

The higher-profile shortfalls listed in the HPC included carrier-based air power, sea-based theatre-missile defence, SEAD aircraft, cruise missiles, precision-guided munitions, air surveillance, attack and reconnaissance helicopters, medium and heavy support helicopters, light infantry and multiple-launch rocket systems. Early-warning and distant-detection requirements (UAVs, AWACS and airborne early warning, airborne ground surveillance and intelligence satellites), sealift, airlift and amphibious shipping were also highlighted as acute gaps. Other shortfalls included special-operations forces, NBC battalions, psychological operations and electronic warfare. There were also gaps in less spectacular areas, such as transport, general support logistics, medical units, recovery and maintenance, engineering, signals and surveillance and target-acquisition units, and a shortage of military observers and military police.

The Capability Improvement Conference

The HPC paved the way for the November 2001 EU Capability Improvement Conference, which pledged to address the flaws it identified. Although the Western European states made additional contributions, there was essentially no progress in the areas demanding major procurements.

Significant acquisitions and procurements cannot be changed overnight – most acquisitions take several years to plan and finance and major projects can take a decade or more to develop and produce. No matter what the political process or Headline Goal may demand, assets such as strategic airlift, satellites or communications equipment will not be developed or financed in the space of a few years. Besides, as long as most European states feel secure and crisis management is not seen as a matter of defending vital interests, developing capability for distant autonomous high-tech enforcement operations will not be given priority (unless of course it is a question of national prestige, industries or jobs).

At the 2001 conference, member states committed more than 100,000 soldiers, some 400 aircraft and 100 ships. In quantitative terms, levels increased from those reached at the 2000 commitment conference, and gaps relating to bridging-engineer units, electronic warfare and multiple rocket launchers were addressed. Gaps not addressed included logistics, force protection, operational and strategic mobility (air and sea), combat search and rescue and precision-guided munitions. Command, control, communications and intelligence capabilities remained of questionable quality, and shortfalls persisted in surveillance and reconnaissance.

The European Capability Action Plan

Further steps were taken in February 2002, when EU member states agreed on a voluntary European Capability Action Plan (ECAP). The ECAP aimed to incorporate all the investment, development and coordination measures executed or planned, both nationally and multinationally, with a view to improving existing resources and gradually developing the capabilities deemed necessary for the EU's activities. It offers a forum for identifying requirements, enhancing multilateral coordination and encouraging national initiatives on capabilities. It specifically states that multinational solutions might include the co-production, financing and acquisition of capabilities, particularly for large-scale projects.

The ECAP establishes a number of panels, each focusing on a specific capability such as strategic airlift, UAVs, air-to-ground missiles or communications. Each panel is chaired by a member state (a 'pilot country') or two, responsible for leading, coordinating and summarising the panel's work. This adds impetus to the whole process since national prestige is at stake. Unfortunately, there is a tendency for member states to focus on projects that they have a direct interest in developing, or to participate in order to minimise the potential damage to other national pet projects. On the other hand, the prospects for coordination are greater than would have been the case without the ECAP.

EU non-military/civilian crisis-management goals

Non-military or civilian instruments of crisis management and conflict prevention were also highlighted at Helsinki, though they were not directly linked to the Headline Goal. In recognition of the EU's comparative advantage in this area, member states agreed that: 'A non-military crisis management mechanism will be established to coordinate and make more effective the various civilian means and resources, in parallel with the military ones, at the disposal of the Union and the Member States.'[25] At the EU summit at Feira in June 2000, the EU decided to focus on four aspects of civilian crisis management: police, the rule of law, civil administration and civil protection.

EU members made it their goal to provide up to 5,000 police officers for international missions by 2003, with 1,000 available at 30 days' notice.[26] The Police Action Plan agreed at the Gothenburg summit in June 2001 called for the establishment of operational headquarters, interoperability criteria, training programmes, the development of interfaces with military and other civilian components of crisis management and the development of a legal framework for police operations (including Status of Forces Agreements). Since then, the development of common concepts, command-and-control arrangements, selection and training criteria and compatible equipment lists and guidelines, for instance for criminal procedure and civilian administration in crisis-management operations, has made significant progress. The EU has even been able to offer the UN help in improving its guidelines, for example in the rule-of-law field. This development of common European standards and training will eventually enhance internal police and civil-emergency cooperation within the EU.

The Ministerial Police Capabilities Commitment Conference in November 2001 received commitments for 5,000 police officers for crisis-management operations by 2003 – though remarkably without any explicit reference to the changed international environment after 11 September. Of these, 1,400 will be deployable within 30 days. By any measure, this is a major undertaking. The EU police capability is meant to cover the full range of missions, from training, advice and monitoring to executive tasks. In 2003, the EU is to take over the UN police mission in Bosnia, with almost 500 officers. Even if the pledged numbers are available as promised – which is not yet fully the case – it is not certain whether the available assets will be adequate to the task at hand, and whether their deployment will be given sufficient political and financial importance by the states sending them. Language requirements as well as the reluctance of national police forces to make their core personnel available for international missions are further complicating factors.

The development of *gendarmerie*-type heavy police has made little progress on the European level, but further headway is likely as more European states acknowledge the value of such capabilities for counter-terrorist operations and engagements where traditional police forces are too weak and military combat forces too provocative or expensive. It is likely that the impact of 11 September will in the long run lead to a number of new forms of European internal-security and police cooperation, perhaps including integrated border controls and coast-guard forces.[27]

During the first half of 2001, civilian crisis management overshadowed the military elements of the ESDP, and the scope of EU crisis management and conflict prevention was significantly broadened, in some eyes beyond the traditional Petersberg range. Members committed themselves to an additional pool of 200 officials for crisis-management operations (judges, prosecutors and correction/penitentiary officers) to supplement the police. The pledging conference in May 2002 actually exceeded this target, with a total pledge of 282 officials. Lead elements are to be deployable within 30 days. The basic idea behind such rule-of-law missions is to ensure that the area of operations has a complete and functioning criminal-justice process. Although these missions will most likely complement police operations, the capability could in theory be deployed on its own, or with other EU capabilities.

EU members also agreed to create a pool of experts in civil administration, ranging from elections and taxation to health services and waste management, and to establish a 2,000-strong civil-protection capability for major natural, technological and environmental emergencies. Key functions would include search and rescue, the construction of refugee camps, logistical support and communications. Although not envisaged at the time, EU states' civil-protection capabilities will also be relevant in the wake of large-scale terrorist attacks. EU member states had already decided at Gothenburg to develop common standards and modules for training, and common exercises.

By the EU Summit in Seville in June 2002, further progress had been made in implementing the Police Action Plan and in civil protection/emergency relief. The non-military aspects of ESDP became more prominent, and the link between civilian and military crisis-management capabilities was reinforced. The EU also reaffirmed that it was prepared to take over the UN police mission in Bosnia from January 2003. Member states agreed that the development of the ESDP and Headline Goal must take fuller account of the capabilities that may be required to combat terrorism. These include enhancing EU instruments for long-term conflict prevention, political dialogue with third countries, non-proliferation and arms control, and providing assistance to third countries so that they can increase their capacity to respond to terrorism. The EU also plans to include anti-terrorism clauses in EU agreements with third countries and to re-evaluate relations in the light of these countries' attitudes towards terrorism. However, although counter-terrorism falls within the realm of the Common Foreign and Security Policy (CFSP), it is questionable whether it can be regarded as part of the ESDP under the 1992 definition of the Petersberg spectrum of tasks. Arguably, counter-terrorism may affect territorial issues and states' self-defence, which do not come under the ESDP – at least for now.

Interim modalities for financing EU crisis-management operations have also been agreed. In principle, the EC budget will pay for institutional administrative costs, while operational expenditures for national military forces engaged in the operation are paid for by the troop-contributing nation. This is the same principle that NATO has used for years. The Council will decide on a case-by-case basis whether deployment and lodging expenses should be regarded as a common or a national cost. Individual states are responsible for deploying and sustaining forces in crisis-management operations. There has been debate over whether the EU should have a separate budget for common costs relating to crisis-management operations, and whether a start-up fund for operations should be established.

EU structures for security and defence cooperation

In parallel with these capability initiatives, developing security and defence cooperation within the EU has also required structural change. In 1999, EU member states agreed to establish new working bodies. These were set up in March 2000, and made permanent in January 2001. They included:

- the post of Secretary-General of the Council of the European Union/High Representative (SG/HR) for the Common Foreign and Security Policy (CFSP) – filled by Javier Solana – and the associated SG/HR Policy Unit;
- the Political and Security Committee (comparable to NATO's North Atlantic Council (NAC));
- the Committee for Civilian Aspects of Crisis Management;
- the Military Committee;
- the Military Staff; and
- a Police Unit in the Council Secretariat as part of the Police Action Plan.

A Joint Situation Centre (SITCEN) was also established, with an embryonic intelligence and assessment cell. This has since developed and grown, with an increased capability to manage intelligence from member states. It has even started to assign tasks to national intelligence services, either informally or, on a voluntary basis, formally. To an extent, the SITCEN can produce its own assessments and analyses in support of the Council and the Council Secretariat. Input from the EU Military Committee, and above all the 120-strong Military Staff, has meant that the quality of concepts, procedures and structures for coordinating crisis management within the EU has vastly improved. The formal mission of the Military Staff is to perform 'early warning, situation assessment and strategic planning for Petersberg tasks',[28] to provide military expertise and to conduct EU-led military crisis-management operations.[29]

The Political and Security Committee, which is subordinate to the EU Council, deals with all aspects of the EU's foreign and security policy, including the ESDP. It is the focal point for crisis management. During EU operations, it will exercise political control and provide strategic direction. With the exception of EU operations, the Political and Security Committee is not a decision-making body, though it is the prime decision-*shaping* organ in the CFSP/ESDP realm.

Additional forums have also been established, such as the EU Headline Goal Task Force, a Working Group on Capabilities and the Politico-Military Working Group.[30] Since the attacks in the US in September 2001, ESDP institutions have also fed into assessments of the terrorist threat, and have contributed to the Political and Security Committee's position. ESDP processes, procedures and structures were tested in early 2002 in a crisis-management exercise involving Brussels and all EU member states. One of the main lessons of the exercise, the first of its kind in the EU, was the need for stronger civil–military coordination.

The transatlantic capabilities debate and the Prague Summit

Both the US and NATO international staffs have encouraged the Europeans to develop their military capabilities. The reaction in most European capitals has, however, been lukewarm. For most European governments, increasing defence expenditures or signing on to expensive procurement projects that do not benefit domestic employment or growth is not an option. Moreover, while the US may have a clear conception of current threats and what they mean in terms of capabilities, most Europeans have not significantly changed their views on either since the 1990s. For the US, the standard is still US defence spending, US interests and US global commitments and ambitions. The problem is that, whatever initiatives the US comes up with for its NATO allies, defence spending and national procurement are determined by parliaments, governments and the shape of domestic politics within individual countries. It is nonetheless true, as NATO Secretary-General Lord Robertson argues, that the Europeans are still spending enormous amounts of money on capabilities that the US and NATO believe they do not need. It is also true that Europeans hesitate to buy US products in areas such as strategic airlift, communications and precision-guided munitions because this offers little benefit to European defence industries, even if these US alternatives are often cheaper, more advanced and readily available 'off-the-shelf'.

For many Europeans, the normal NATO defence planning process, as opposed to fast-track initiatives *à la* the DCI, appear sufficient as a mechanism for developing interoperability and new capabilities. In this context, the ESDP's role in defence planning has been difficult to grasp. The EU's review mechanism, the Capability Development Mechanism (CDM), the collective name for the permanent process that sets in once a political Headline Goal is set, mirrors NATO's process. It is geared towards identifying required capabilities, getting member states to commit to them, and then monitoring progress and addressing shortfalls. A working interface between EU and NATO activities in this area is essential if unnecessary and unhelpful duplication is to be avoided. However, some Europeans hope that, by using EU defence planning through the CDM and the ECAP, US involvement and pressure can be kept to a minimum. Certain EU governments have been more comfortable discussing procurement and capabilities development in this forum, rather than in NATO. Some European governments have stressed their preference to look beyond traditional military capabilities and take a more comprehensive view of security and the projection of security to crisis regions, to encompass elements such as aid, confidence-building, state-building and police or *gendarmerie* operations. This approach is in part based on experiences in the Balkans, and also reflects deep differences with the US over the threat posed by terrorism, ballistic-missile attacks and weapons of mass destruction, as well as the nature of relations with countries such as Libya, Iran and Iraq.

In this context, it is worth noting what the Europeans have signed up to in NATO. In a Statement on Capabilities, agreed by NATO defence ministers in June 2002, member states acknowledged that the capacity of the alliance to carry out the full range of its missions will depend largely on its ability to 'increase substantially' the proportion of combat and support forces available for out-of-area deployment, or where there is little or no host-nation support. Future capabilities should focus on defending against chemical, biological, radiological and nuclear attacks, secure command communications and information superiority, interoperability and the rapid deployment and sustainment of combat forces. NATO states also agreed to encourage 'the pooling of military capabilities, increasing role specialisation, cooperative acquisition of equipment and multinational funding'.[31] Change is, however, likely to be slow, and it will be several years before the impact is felt on NATO force planning.

NATO's Prague Summit in November 2002 seemed set to follow past patterns. The Prague Capabilities Commitment, launched by the US and the NATO Secretary General, set out the following aims:

- to equip all deployable NATO forces, with 30 days' or higher readiness, with chemical, biological, radiological and nuclear defence;
- to complete, by 2004, the design and development phase of NATO airborne Ground Surveillance (reconnaissance and targeting support);
- to develop a full set of deployable and secure command, control and communications capabilities for deployable HQs;
- to increase the number of precision-guided munitions by 30% by 2005;
- to increase SEAD capabilities by 50% by 2005;
- to increase the alliance's strategic airlift and air-tanker capabilities by 50% by 2004; and
- to increase deployable logistics and combat-service support capabilities by 25% by 2005.[32]

Although many of the above increases are substantial in relative terms, one must remember the real starting point which is often less impressive. Significantly, the process generated two new formulas that should be applauded, whatever the institutional label. The first is a pool of jointly-owned and operated support jamming pods for electronic warfare, an air-to-air refuelling fleet and UAVs. The second idea is for Europe to lease 10–12 US C-17 aircraft (or equivalents) until the delivery of the Airbus A400M by the end of the decade. Obviously, this 'wish list' will not materialise in full, even if the new formulas were accepted by European states. It all costs money, which most European defence budgets do not have.

At the summit, the US also launched a new NATO Response Force (NRF). The idea is that NATO needs a multinational joint force for primarily out-of-area operations, with immediate readiness (5–30 days).[33] The force is to be operational by 2006. Tasks are similar to the EU Headline Goal, and include non-combatant evacuation operations, proactive force projection and serving as an initial entry force for a large-scale operation. The US emphasis is however on joint high-intensity combat outside Europe. According to the proposal, the force is to comprise around 20,000 soldiers, with a brigade-sized land component. In its expeditionary nature, there are similarities between the new US Interim Brigade Combat Team (which is under development) and the NRF's land component. The Combined Joint Task Force (CJTF) HQs would be suitable for the NRF. The idea is that the NRF would set a new standard for European military capabilities. The need for strategic airlift, air refuelling, secure command and control and precision-guided munitions for the European elements of the NRF would be clear and European governments would be challenged to set the necessary priorities. The side benefit would be a new US–European project, with increased military cooperation and interoperability.[34]

The sum of the initiatives

According to US Senator Jesse Helms, former Chairman of the Senate Committee on Foreign Relations, the EU 'could not fight its way out of a wet paper bag'.[35] Former British Prime Minister Margaret Thatcher has called the Headline Goal a 'monumental folly' designed to 'satisfy political vanity', with 'no military sense at all'.[36]

Europe's capabilities are not quite that bad, and the EU Headline Goal and enhanced crisis-management capabilities are reasonable and logical from the point of view of almost all Western governments. Both for Europe and for future military and security cooperation between the EU and the US, not to mention Western conflict prevention, many benefits could be derived from a successful ESDP and EU/NATO capabilities initiatives pursued with determination. After having identified the capability gaps, and after having declared that Europe will be able to do more, Europe has little choice but to deliver. By late 2002, key structures were in place and the stage was set for measurable improvements. Significant challenges still remain, but there is little doubt that Europeans will eventually adjust and increase their military and non-military crisis-management capabilities. When, by how much and against which threats remain to be seen.

Chapter 2

Developing the EU's Instruments for Managing International Crises

This chapter analyses the Headline Goal and the EU's development of scenarios for the forces committed to it, as well as other elements of crisis management such as decision-making, planning and intelligence capabilities, and civilian capabilities. Together, these components constitute the current palette of EU assets and capabilities for conflict prevention and crisis management; in essence, this is the EU's contribution to the security dimension of Europe's strategic partnership with the US.

Assessing the Headline Goal

Like many ESDP initiatives, the Headline Goal is essentially a compromise between the UK and France. This does not make it less important, although it does help to explain the sometimes ambiguous and challenging formulations it uses. Although the Goal is set for the end of 2003, it reflects the priorities of 1999, the lessons and frustrations that followed the Kosovo crisis and the challenges Europe faced in deploying yet another large formation to the Balkans. The quantitative goal also reflects the Balkans experience. It is set at corps level (60,000 troops or up to 15 brigades), plus air and naval elements.

Size is not the major problem. The challenges relating to the Headline Goal concern sustainability (specified at one year), readiness (set at 60 days), combat intensity and complexity and self-sustainability. The Headline Goal was not formulated for major high-intensity warfare with a whole corps plus naval and air capabilities on the other side of the globe. The level of ambition is much more modest and, given existing capabilities, more realistic.

One-year sustainability

Depending on the other commitments of nations contributing to the European military operation, the availability and rotation of troops will be challenging. Sustaining 60,000 soldiers for one year engages at least 120,000 troops on the ground *plus* air and naval elements.[1] Depending on the specific mission and the amount of air and naval assets required, the total EU commitment for a one-year operation could engage perhaps 180,000–240,000 men and women in uniform. Moreover, for each half-year rotation, units are 'booked' for 18 months, and cannot be used for other operations.[2]

For an operation longer than one year, the total number of ground forces required for sustaining a corps-size operation would probably be at least 240,000. This is a four-to-one ratio for ground forces, but recent UN and NATO operations, and more than ten years of Balkan peace-support operations for most European armed forces, suggest that even this is insufficient for longer-term sustainment. Again, significant air and naval elements must be added, giving a total sum of perhaps around 350,000 European soldiers, airmen and sailors needed to sustain a joint operation more than one year. It is easy to forget that deployed soldiers are not mere statistics, but individuals with families, military careers and opportunities outside the military. Most units also have duties at home and training requirements for operations other than EU crisis management. In short, the Headline Goal is no small commitment, and will involve a substantial portion of Europe's assets and military capabilities.

As in most cases of crisis management, sustainability is more or less a question of national priorities. Without drawing down existing military crisis-management commitments, and based on the availability of non-engaged rapid-reaction forces in Europe throughout the 1990s, few EU members apart from the UK and France will be able to produce more than a minor, perhaps even a symbolic, additional mid to long term commitment in the next five years or so. Particularly challenging will be the sustainability of forces that are already in short supply, such as logistics, engineers, medical services, helicopter crews and other specialists. Should the operation take place in a climate zone such as a desert or tropical environment, availability would be even more constricted, whatever the formal Headline Goal commitment. Finnish, Danish, Dutch or Hungarian taxpayers would hardly accept keeping a significant portion of their armed forces trained and equipped for desert or jungle warfare.

Sixty-day readiness[3]

The stated high-end commitment is that the EU will be able to deploy up to 60,000 troops in theatre, beyond Europe, within 60 days from an EU Council order to deploy. It took longer than 60 days for NATO, with the full support of US strategic lift, to deploy a corps-sized formation to Albania and Macedonia in 1999; 1,751 airlift missions were involved, together with the movement of 78,000 tonnes of supplies and 42,380 passengers by air and sea.[4]

If there is little warning and the bulk of European forces are engaged in major international operations or have important duties at home, EU member states will most likely not be able to field a large contingent at such short notice, unless it is merely a question of relabelling an already-established force. Should commercial air- and sealift be inappropriate or unavailable, and US airlift not wanted or not available, EU member states will have difficulty quickly deploying forces several thousand kilometres away. Although with a couple of months' warning many of these deployment challenges can be managed. Besides, not all crises will be conveniently located near main airports or harbours.

The mechanisms and arrangements for deploying a major force, and transforming individual national contributions into a combined and joint fighting force, do not yet exist, nor will they be developed overnight. In other words, getting forces from A to B in time is one thing; achieving an effective and coordinated multinational fighting force in such a short time is another.

Combat intensity and complexity

The Headline Goal states that forces will be capable of the full range of Petersberg tasks. Although the scope of these tasks is open to debate, as of 2002 the most demanding is peace enforcement in a non-permissive environment. This means that Europe should be capable of using force on a par with the Anglo-French Rapid Reaction Force in August–September 1995 in central Bosnia during *Operation Deliberate Force*, but on a larger scale and against two parties at the same time. On the other hand, it does not mean that a European operation would necessarily adopt a similar operational tempo, targeting policy or risk level as NATO's *Operation Allied Force* or other US-led military operations.[5] For European forces, combat intensity up to and including peace-enforcement scenarios is not a problem. Most European forces, mainly thanks to a decade of crisis management in the Balkans, are also well prepared for complex situations, ranging from shifting tension levels, civil–military interaction and multinationality down to the lower tactical level.

Self-sustainability

The Headline Goal force should be 'militarily self-sustaining with the necessary command, control and intelligence capabilities, logistics [and] other combat support services'.[6] In other words, it must be self-sufficient and have all the intelligence, transport and command-and-control capabilities it needs for peace-enforcement operations. Today there are serious flaws in these areas. Questions arise over what individual European governments and their armed forces will demand as the minimum level of these capabilities for a high-end, high-risk operation.

Summary of the Headline Goal

The Headline Goal is primarily a political project; at least at this early stage in the ESDP, it is as much the result of political frustration, the dynamics of integration and national defence-industrial interests as it is an expression of the wish to enhance member states' crisis-management capability *per se*. There is an understanding within the EU and in individual member states that the Headline Goal will be realised, whatever assets and capabilities Europeans possess when they are faced with a crisis. The decision to focus on the Petersberg tasks reflects the lowest common denominator among the EU member states, and most European governments have their own domestic interpretation of what the Headline Goal is, how it should be developed and towards what long-term political goal. On the other hand, setting a target and then moving towards it, not an uncommon method in the EU, has proved a successful way of developing the Union. The Headline Goal will probably be updated as the ESDP and European requirements evolve.

US support and access to NATO assets and capabilities

There is an assumption that, in the event of a crisis that demands European action, the US or others may support some European states bilaterally. Faced with a crisis that Europe cannot effectively manage, the European states would then either accept US support bilaterally or through arrangements in NATO, or would redefine 'European' interests, policies and operational ambitions downwards. The Europeans have little choice but to be pragmatic and realistic when it comes to an actual military engagement. However, for all high-end and militarily difficult tasks, or for tasks that clearly lie beyond the Petersberg spectrum, there is a general assumption in European capitals that NATO or a US-led coalition will be the natural choice.

Counting on US engagement, or EU–US cooperation, would save the EU from exposing its immediate capability flaws, and allow the Europeans more time to enhance their capabilities. The basic argument is that the general imperatives of US influence and NATO's *raison d'être* will ensure US engagement in any major crisis in the European area. In most global crisis management, and particularly in crises where even the Europeans are prepared to go to war, it is assumed that both Europe (or at least a selection of Europeans) and the US share common interests. The problem with this assumption is that a strong-minded European NATO member, for reasons relating to the EU or for the sake of national prestige, could block NATO from taking the lead, or lending collective assets. Alternatively, the US might choose not to be involved in European crisis management because of other geographical or political priorities, including homeland defence. Another possibility is that EU states may simply choose not to engage under the EU banner, after rephrasing their collective interests in the given case, as happened in the African Great Lakes contingency in 1996 and 1997. Besides, coalitions-of-the-willing will always remain an option.

In 1996, the NAC agreed to what came to be known as the 'Berlin package'. To develop the European Security and Defence Identity (ESDI) within NATO, using the formula 'separable but not separate capabilities', NATO would support the WEU with planning and command arrangements and other assets and capabilities.[7] The 1999 NATO summit expanded the Berlin package into 'Berlin plus', which gave 'assured EU access to NATO planning capabilities' and ensured the 'presumption of availability to the EU of pre-identified NATO capabilities and common assets'. It also developed the role of the Deputy Supreme Allied Commander Europe (DSACEUR) in order to support European command options.[8]

There were four main motives behind Berlin plus. First, the Europeans asked for access. This reflected their acceptance that their operational capabilities were insufficient, and that they there-fore had to borrow from the alliance. At the EU summit in Nice in 2000, the EU requested access only to 'collective' NATO assets and capabilities. Second, it was an effort to enhance direct EU–NATO cooperation. For the US, this would prevent the creation of a separate European SHAPE, and ensured that EU operations were conducted in accordance with NATO doctrine.[9] Third, there was recognition in Europe of the US argument that establishing separate EU planning assets would damage NATO. Fourth, it was a way for the US, Turkey and other non-EU NATO members to ensure that they were not sidelined in any EU operation – not least in the political deliberations ahead of and during an operation. By main-taining control over NATO assets and capabilities, non-EU states could still have influence and a role. Such EU–NATO arrange-ments are, however, controversial, and highly politicised.

In the 'Berlin-plus' arrangement, where the EU would be assured of access to NATO assets and capabilities, access was highly probable, but not guaranteed. This issue was widely de-bated within NATO. France, for reasons of EU autonomy and for fear of institutionalising what is seen as the EU's dependence on NATO and the US, raised objections to giving the EU guaranteed access to NATO planning capabilities. NATO's International Staff argued that the alliance could only promise 'assured access' because planning staff might become overloaded with requests from the EU, as well as from NATO. Turkey, as a non-EU European member of NATO, has been trying to translate 'assured access' into a guarantee of Turkish involvement in ESDP operations. Despite a diplomatic formula brokered by the US and UK in late 2001, this issue continued to block full implementation of the assured-access approach because Greece, which is in both the EU and NATO, made its agreement conditional on Turkish concessions regarding Cyprus, and is adamantly against increased Turkish influence in the EU. From the viewpoint of the US and most European governments, NATO's guarantee of operational-planning support to the EU is essential for preventing an EU attempt to create its own capabilities outside the NATO framework.

NATO planning

NATO defence planning coordinates national forces and capabilities to attain common goals. The planning cycle includes Ministerial Guidance (strategic goals), Force Proposals (force targets, essentially formulated by NATO military staff in consultation with individual member states), Force Goals (proposals adopted by individual members) and a mechanism for peer review and progress assessment of the national goals.[10] Although this process has been important in setting common goals and in building confidence among NATO members, it is slow and cumbersome. There is poor coordination between the various functions and capabilities, no guarantee that nations will fulfil their commitments and there is room for reform. In reality, few states are prepared to have their priorities dictated externally, and national defence ministries are keen to ensure that force goals match what they planned to do anyway – and maybe even manage to get some NATO support for the project.

One component of the Berlin-plus formula was that NATO's defence-planning system should incorporate forces for EU-led operations. However, perceptions among NATO states as to what this means clearly diverge. Some argue that it is a question of including EU 'defence planning' in NATO defence planning, while others see this as an opportunity for NATO to modify its outdated and less-than-effective planning process. If NATO defence planning had been truly effective in the past, there would not have been the need for initiatives such as the DCI and the Prague Capabilities Commitment. Moreover, in Europe there would be less duplication of national assets in areas such as air-defence fighters, main battle tanks, submarines and operational staff. Defence planning continues to reflect national political priorities, not collective needs or rational cooperation. Even with future initiatives to reenergise or rationalise NATO defence planning, the priorities of national governments, and ultimately the taxpayers, are likely to prevail.

Operational planning within NATO (as opposed to defence planning) consists of contingency operations plans (COPs), concepts of operations (CONOPS) and operations plans (OPLANS). As of 2002 the Combined Joint Planning Staff (CJPS), SACEUR and the Supreme Allied Commander Atlantic (SACLANT) produced these plans at the strategic level. NATO's International Staff and International Military Staff also contribute to elements of operational planning. There is extensive expertise at NATO headquarters in planning European military crisis-management operations.[11] The Combined Joint Planning Staff has been the key developer of ESDI-related concepts and has done a significant amount of work on the CJTFs and in support of the WEU. It has a formal role to provide support for ESDI/WEU operational planning.

During 2000 and 2001, the DSACEUR, Rupert Smith, and SHAPE took extraordinary steps to open NATO operational and defence planning to the EU. NATO International Staff and the US advocated a far-reaching EU–NATO collaborative defence-planning process, including all EU and NATO member states. There were also plans to open up SHAPE to all EU states. The official reason for this was to minimise duplication, but the underlying purpose was US and NATO concern that the alternative would pave the way for a separate EU defence-planning process, and separate EU operational planning, which could split NATO. The Combined Joint Planning Staff would play a complementary role as the prime operational planner for European military crisis management, including EU-led operations without any operational support from NATO.

There are essentially four options for EU–NATO operational cooperation. The first is for the EU to rely on NATO operational planning and command structures using DSACEUR and/or a CJTF headquarters, and perhaps other capabilities such as AWACS. This option, where the EU would only provide political leadership and strategic direction, would probably be the most effective from a war-fighting and command-and-control perspective. A second option would be to employ NATO operational planning and some NATO capabilities, while using a European operational headquarters and a non-NATO chain of command. This combination could create considerable difficulties if, for instance, US support for the EU operation was placed under the operational command of a French force commander and operational headquarters. The third option is for the EU to rely on NATO operational planning without using NATO structures or capabilities in the operation. This would demand close coordination between, for example, the Combined Joint Planning Staff and the European operational headquarters. There is also the option of EU autonomous engagement, whereby the EU does not rely on NATO operational planning or military capabilities. The UK and France and their national joint operational planning HQs would play lead roles here.

Collective NATO assets

For all the debate and posturing within NATO and the EU over providing NATO assets and capabilities, the alliance actually has relatively few collective assets, and not all of them can be categorised as capabilities for crisis-management operations. In 2002, the alliance collectively had 18 AWACS, 20 stationary headquarters, two not-yet-fully operational CJTF headquarters, a research ship and a pipeline system (mainly for jet fuel). Individual member states owned all the other assets assigned or linked to NATO. SHAPE, together with the Combined Joint Planning Staff, would probably be classified as a capability that could assist an EU operation, not an asset that could be placed under EU command.

Of these collective assets and capabilities, the AWACS and staff elements from established headquarters are of most interest for EU-led military crisis management. The CJTF headquarters have become large, heavy and US-dominated, and seem to be less attractive as lead elements for EU-led operations. NATO has no deployable land or maritime component headquarters or strategic and tactical intelligence capabilities – requirements that EU states say they need for EU operations. For operations in 2003 and 2004, NATO as such has little to offer the EU in terms of operational capabilities. It is a myth that the EU and its member states are dependant on NATO assets and capabilities; these are useful, rather than essential, as individual European states already have much of what is needed, including AWACS, deployable headquarters and intelligence capabilities.

Inside NATO, the 'presumption of availability' of pre-identified capabilities and assets does not constitute a binding commitment, and decisions will be made by the NAC on a case-by-case basis. This is a weak link that may well be exploited by an opponent. With regard to national assets and capabilities, it is up to the EU, or more likely individual EU member states, to conclude bilateral agreements for loan, lease or support. Here, cooperation with the US naturally plays a central role.

What if the definition of NATO assets and capabilities expanded to include NATO formations such as the standing naval forces, the Allied Command Europe Rapid Reaction Corps (ARRC), the NATO Response Force or *ad hoc* formations? Every government of participating forces in such a formation would still have to approve any participation, naturally on a case-by-case basis. A NATO force could however be coordinated inside the NATO framework and collectively offered to the EU. The 'NATO label' *per se* would have little or no operational significance – although the political signal could be substantial (giving headlines such as 'NATO airlift task force supports the EU Operation' or 'EU force evacuated by NATO special forces'). It is most likely that a 'NATO label' would be used by the US in order to spread the political and operational risk, accentuate the role and vitality of NATO, and strengthen EU–NATO links.

Once there is agreement for NATO or NATO-coordinated support for an EU operation, what happens if the alliance or individual states providing 'NATO support' change their minds in the middle of the operation, or after a long commitment? For example, what happens if an EU operation evolves in a direction that does not suit the US, which has provided intelligence and transport via NATO? Could compelling national reasons lead the US to pull officers out of NATO headquarters lent to the EU operation? The impact of this would be mostly political and in terms of alliance cohesion, but there could still be serious operational ramifications.

There is also a difficult question around who would pay for the operational use of NATO assets or capabilities in EU-led operations. There is no reason why the allies should collectively foot the bill – especially since the collective NATO budget is tiny.[12] Would the EU collectively pay for the NATO asset or capability, or would this be handled on a bilateral basis? Who would pay if, for example, a NATO AWACS were shot down while supporting an EU-led operation? Another issue is the potential escalation of an EU-led operation into a NATO collective-defence operation.

Should DSACEUR (a British or German officer) be designated by the EU and NATO members as the Operation Commander or Force Commander, many formal difficulties would be avoided. By being able to play both the European and NATO card, the prospects for using the best assets and capabilities from both organisations is relatively bright. However, the role of DSACEUR *vis-à-vis* EU crisis management has been politicised, and will probably remain sensitive for some time to come.

Assessing the EU's scenarios

While NATO military crisis management will take place only on a case-by-case basis, the EU has a permanent role in promoting stability through economic, political and military policies. The EU has no geographical restrictions.[13] Although EU experience is grounded in the Balkans, operations in Asia or Africa are often mentioned as examples of future EU crisis management, and there is the option of using the forces committed to the Headline Goal in international UN operations. In addition, both the EU and NATO can lend support to international coalitions outside the formal EU or NATO framework.

Scenario development

The potentially wide scope of action and national interests among the key European players has complicated the process of identifying scenarios for the forces committed to the Headline Goal. As there was no agreement in the wake of the Helsinki meeting in 1999, the path of least resistance led the EU to adopt three of the WEU's Illustrated Profiles (that is, military scenarios – the same as those used in assessing the WEU Audit of Assets). The scenarios are therefore based on traditional peace-support operations of the 1990s, and are relatively conventional in nature. That does not mean that the scenarios will not be modified over time, or that new ones focusing on, for example, civil protection, civil crisis-management or counter-terrorism, will not eventually complement this traditional scope.

While the existing scenarios do not provide a sound basis for realistic operational planning or identifying needs, they do demonstrate EU member states' level of ambition and the national political interests in play. There was a strong correlation between the force requirements for the scenarios and what EU members in 1999–2002 were prepared to offer in the first place. For many, it was important that the scenarios and the subsequent force requirements reflected EU power-projection capability and/ or already identified procurement demands: the A400M transport aircraft, aircraft carriers, intelligence satellites and UAVs, cruise missiles, attack helicopters, multiple-launch rocket systems and other pet national projects. Assets had to be 'tailored' to European needs and European scenarios to safeguard the interests of European defence industries. Buying American assets, or depending on US capabilities, was not seen as an option in many EU capitals. Some states argued that the scenarios should be small and manageable, in order not to challenge NATO's primacy, the US role in Europe and/or national defence budgets. Others saw the scenarios as a way of pressing ahead with radical defence restructuring, increasing military capabilities, maximising national defence industrial interests or increasing defence expenditure. Even within EU states, national defence, finance and foreign ministries had very different ambitions with regard to the scenarios.

On the one hand, the US supported ambitious EU goals in order to force Europeans to fulfil the DCI, assume more of the burden in Europe and enhance Europe's ability to cooperate with the US in safeguarding mutual interests beyond the continent. On the other hand, the US did not want to encourage the ESDP and competition with NATO. US defence industrial interests were also at work. France also wanted more ambitious objectives, but to reinforce European autonomy; there was, for instance, heated debate on how many combat aircraft the EU needed for the most demanding scenario, with the French calling for a force comparable with *Operation Allied Force*, and the US and more cautious European states arguing for around half that.

On several occasions, NATO operational planners (who largely developed the EU scenarios and calculated which capabilities were needed) came up with results that EU capitals did not like. For instance, one scenario called for more forces or longer deployment times than permitted by the Headline Goal. In response, the parameters were simply changed: harbours were enlarged (the tiny port of Durrës grew to Rotterdam-like size), the quality of roads improved (dirt roads became multi-lane highways), or the level of hostilities reduced to fit member states' interests and policies.[14] This resulted in the development of scenarios that were less than realistic, and of limited value as a basis for operational planning.

The 'Assistance to Civilians' scenario

The 'Assistance to Civilians' scenario dealt with refugee flows, humanitarian aid and the evacuation of EU nationals at a distance of 10,000 km from Brussels. The environment was largely permissive, but enforcement measures could be required. The reaction time would be short. The scenario resembled *Operation Alba* in 1997 or a small UNPROFOR, and tasks included area security and ensuring freedom of movement, information operations, humanitarian assistance and providing support for international agencies and evacuation operations.

The land component would require a divisional force of up to 9,000 troops (with a pool of 60,000 should the need arise), and would include armoured troops, mechanised infantry, air-mobile and armoured cavalry, artillery, special forces and psychological-operations troops. The air component would call for defensive counter-air, SEAD and close air support. Supporting air assets would include AWACS aircraft, air-to-air refuelling and combat search and rescue. Electronic intelligence, signals intelligence and airborne command, control and communications (ABCCC) and electronic-warfare forces would also be required. Maritime assets would range from carrier battle groups and amphibious shipping to submarines.

The 'Conflict Prevention/Preventive Deployment' scenario

The 'Conflict Prevention/Preventive Deployment' scenario called for expeditious and firm enforcement of a peace settlement. The scenario put the crisis at 4,000 km from Brussels. The environment was again permissive, but the force had to be capable of enforcement and securing the region. Police and civilian support would complement the corps-sized military element. This scenario implied that the EU should control a crisis area, thus paving the way for a peace process and the return of displaced people and refugees. The scenario could be compared with IFOR/SFOR, or KFOR after 1999. The forces required included a military police brigade, eight combat brigades, carrier battle groups and amphibious groups, UAVs, electronic intelligence and a considerable strategic reserve.

The 'Separation of Parties by Force' scenario

This was the most demanding scenario.[15] It required the EU to occupy a region 4,000 km from Brussels, and force two warring parties to accept a dictated peace. The environment was non-permissive and the risk high. The war-like situation precluded civil–military cooperation. Although *Operation Deliberate Force* in Bosnia in August–September 1995 was not as complex, dangerous or large, it gives an impression of the EU scenario.[16] The scenario is thus more demanding than the IFOR entry operation in autumn 1995, or the KFOR entry operation in June 1999.

The corps-level land force (60,000 troops plus 3,400 for an emergency evacuation operation) would include some 17 brigades, nine of which would be manoeuvre brigades (plus artillery, air-defence and support brigades). The force would also have attack helicopters. Although the scenario was 'land-heavy', the air component would be extensive, requiring up to 300 aircraft. It would be offensive in nature, and include all-weather strike capabilities, SEAD, offensive air and close air support, electronic warfare and ABCCC elements. The maritime component, requiring some 75 ships, would be diverse in order to deal with sea control, maritime embargo and air support for amphibious forces. The scenario called for substantial strategic reserves.

There were discrepancies between the NATO input and the proposed Force Requirements and those adopted by the EU ahead of the Capabilities Commitment Conference. NATO's technical advice did not call for intelligence or communication satellites. This may indicate that NATO staff or the US did not want to provide clear support for French and/or German satellite developments that would decrease European dependence on the US. The size and weight of the forces needed for the high-end scenario imply that Europe would be dependent on the US for several assets, such as heavy strategic airlift capable of transporting tanks. Furthermore, Europe will not own ABCCC or major combat search and rescue capabilities, or sufficient SEAD, precision-guided munitions and air-to-air refuelling for a large operation on a par with US/NATO speed and risk levels by 2003. It would be in the United States' and NATO's interest to persuade the Europeans to acquire such assets and capabilities.

EU decision-making, planning and intelligence capabilities

The EU's assets and capabilities for autonomous strategic decision-making, planning and intelligence are scarce. This is a limiting factor in conflict prevention, crisis management and cooperation with the US.[17] Although the EU has a well-established strategic decision-making capability for elements of the First Pillar (EU relations within the CFSP framework), effective decision-making for inter-governmental crisis management is unproven. Processes are still being put in place, and there is unlikely to be a true strategic decision-making capability for crisis management until the EU has engaged in one or two major crises. The role of the EU's

ESDP structures *vis-à-vis* national capitals, and how effective coordination will be between member states, will depend not only on the crisis in question and the varying national interests involved, but also on what added value the common ESDP structures can offer. In relation to the US, effective EU decision-making in the CFSP and ESDP framework is essential. If the EU cannot speak with one voice, and act quickly with cohesion and efficiency in coordinating economic, diplomatic and military elements, it will be a less attractive partner to the US.

For EU-led operations using NATO assets and capabilities, the EU Summit in Nice stated that operational planning would be carried out by NATO (SHAPE and the Combined Joint Planning Staff). In practice, this means that the EU would formally lead the operation, but that NATO would handle all the planning and command arrangements (probably through DSACEUR). US influence would be substantial as long as US and NATO assets were used, and EU autonomy would be nil. Such an arrangement may not be a problem in EU–US or EU–NATO cooperation, but it would be an issue if the EU member states must, or want to, act on their own.

For autonomous EU operations, the EU Military Staff would be tasked with setting the operational parameters at the strategic level.[18] Europe should accordingly develop a capability to plan for the whole spectrum of Petersberg tasks, an objective that will take several years to realise.[19] For any operational planning, the EU Military Staff will have to duplicate substantial parts of the planning elements of SHAPE and the Combined Joint Planning Staff. The EU would rely heavily on British and French operational joint planning capabilities. To manage an EU operation, the EU Military Staff will have to develop structures to link the SG/HR and Political and Security Committee, and indirectly the EU Commission and the member states, to the Operations Commander.[20] Multinationality, where all participating member states have representation at all levels, is not easy and not always especially effective – albeit necessary in EU or alliance operations. For small and relatively simple operations, a tactical headquarters such as the Allied Command Europe Rapid Reaction Corps (ARRC), under the EU flag, or a EUROCORPS augmented with joint expertise and liaison officers, could also play a lead role in operational planning.

Intelligence poses a major challenge. For the foreseeable future, the EU as an institution will not have credible intelligence input or output for strategic decision-making, operational assessments or operational command. Assets and capabilities are essentially limited to the small Joint Situation Centre, the EU Military Staff and the Satellite Centre (with most raw input coming from commercial satellites and the French–Spanish–Italian *Helios I* reconnaissance satellites). Even with the addition of national capabilities, the geographical scope of intelligence gathering and the likely depth of EU-wide assessments will not match the ambitions of the CFSP or the Headline Goal scenarios. Although there is extensive bilateral intelligence cooperation across the Atlantic, and also within Europe, the prospects of US or bilateral intelligence being made directly available to the EU seem remote. EU member states will continue to rely on US intelligence and little will be available at the EU level. EU CFSP/ESDP structures will be dependent on national assessments that have been 'washed' for EU consumption, delivered sporadically and voluntarily. Significant national intelligence is generally only released in the case of a specific threat or crisis, and little is channelled to the EU for more forward-looking pre-crisis conflict prevention, or for potential threats such as terrorism. Thus, current structures and processes are not a basis for strategic decision-making and operational control.

Only when European trust and cooperation enables genuine intelligence sharing among all member states will the EU be able to compete with, and manage relatively well without, US technical assistance for traditional crisis management. In practice, European states have yet to achieve equally close relations with their neighbours in the intelligence field as they have with the US. On the technical side, the small number of European higher-end intelligence sensors, such as satellites, comprise only a fraction of what the EU needs in order to plan and to take decisions autonomously.

European conflict prevention and civilian crisis management

The EU's most influential tools for affecting international stability are non-military, most notably economic measures backed by diplomacy. The EU accounts for 20% of global trade and 30% of the world's industrial production, provides 50% of all humanitarian aid and accounts for 60% of worldwide development aid. When national assets and capabilities are added, the EU has a potentially huge array of tools for projecting stability.[21]

Even before a crisis occurs, the EU can use economic instruments such as trade, tariffs and subsidies, loan policies, foreign aid, refugee management and immigration policy to exert influence. Democracy and human-rights support, arms control, de-mining and state-building are all important. Police missions, diplomatic contacts, defence diplomacy, observer missions, sharing intelligence and promoting the rule of law are also instruments of preventive diplomacy and conflict prevention. Together with other institutions such as the UN and NATO, the combined and coordinated effort of the EU's member states could have a considerable impact. In the case of counter-terrorism in the wake of 11 September, for instance, the EU's broad palette of economic and diplomatic instruments has proved useful and relevant, both for short-term initiatives and for long-term prevention efforts. This does not compete or challenge the US or NATO, or diminish the role of states and bilateral ties.

Emergency relief or civil protection in the wake of natural or man-made disasters is another tool of EU crisis management, which can be applied either within the EU itself, or globally. This element should include both non-military and military capabilities, which should be closely coordinated. Apart from counter-terrorism, threats or challenges such as international crime, drug-trafficking, people-smuggling, the illegal flow of money, goods and people and issues such as technology transfers also demand collective approaches as part of a common foreign and security policy. Many elements of civilian crisis management are equally relevant for internal and external security.

Principal challenges
There are five principal challenges facing EU civilian crisis management. All are manageable, though some will probably only be

dealt with in the face of an acute crisis. Although it is too early to be certain, the events of 11 September may constitute such an event. The EU Convention may also add unexpected momentum in this field.

The first challenge is structural, and relates to the internal rivalry between the European Council, the SG/HR and the European Commission. As in any large organisation, personalities and turf battles have a significant impact on practical cooperation.

The second challenge concerns the functional coordination of the vast array of CFSP/ESDP components across the three EU pillars and the various directorates, secretariats and power-centres. Since some elements, such as counter-terrorism or civil protection, are equally relevant for internal and external security, this could complicate coordination. Furthermore, decision-making procedures and the respective roles of member states and EU organs differ between the EU's various pillars.

Third, few member states have a deep-seated interest in multinational civilian crisis management, and few have a defined policy in this area. Often, civilian crisis management is not high-profile and rarely makes for spectacular headlines. Its success is difficult to measure, and a conflict prevented is essentially a non-event in the eyes of the media and the general public. In relation to other categories of crisis management, conflict prevention will always compete for interest and resources.[22] Above all, there is little domestic support for sending scarce resources such as police officers, doctors, judges, prosecutors, engineers and money elsewhere. An added complication for national coordination is the fact that the assets belong to different ministries, individual federal states, counties and cities. Even with the EU Rapid Reaction Mechanism for financing civilian crisis management, long-term financing would be challenging for most governments. Developing such capabilities is hampered by difficulties in signing contracts with civilians, as there are challenging national training requirements, on-call arrangements and insurance issues. International interoperability and training is yet another problem, and it is often much easier to let non-governmental organisations do the job.

Fourth, there is a general reluctance to link military and civilian assets. Although the WEU made some headway on this point, many European armed forces fear that their professionalism and war-fighting expertise are threatened by further civilian cooperation. Conversely, civilians are sometimes concerned that they will be 'tainted' by involvement with uniformed personnel/combatants. Finally, there is no culture of EU preventive engagement, and the function will remain embryonic for some time.

Chapter 3

A New EU–US Strategic Partnership and Future EU–NATO Relations

The new transatlantic agenda

Between them, the EU and the US are home to 650m people, have a combined gross domestic product (GDP) of over $18,000 billion, representing 58% of world GDP, and account for more than 40% of the international trade in goods and services. In many, perhaps most, aspects of security and defence, including crisis management, the interests of Europeans and Americans coincide, even if policies, values, approaches and priorities may differ.[1]

Formal cooperation between the EU and the US is based on the Transatlantic Declaration of 1990. The New Transatlantic Agenda was adopted in 1995, and a follow-up is in preparation. Points of contact range from summit meetings and senior-level groups to working groups and meetings of experts. Since 1995, the dialogue has developed from consultations towards cooperation and joint action plans. Although a significant portion of the dialogue is on trade, the agenda has for several years included issues like the ESDP, non-proliferation and counter-terrorism, as well as the global challenges of energy, the environment and HIV/AIDS. In all probability, EU–US forums and points of contact will develop into an even closer relationship – particularly where interests and threat perceptions converge.

The US reaction to the ESDP

The US has generally viewed the ESDP and European relations through the lens of NATO.[2] The ESDP has been seen as controversial, and as posing a threat to NATO and US influence in Europe. The debate became particularly lively with the launch of the Headline Goal.[3] EU statements of 'autonomy' and 'self-sustainability', and individual states' talk of European 'first choice', 'emancipation', 'independence' and 'Western bi-polarity', reflected ambitions and visions that could be seen as threatening to the Cold War institutional setting, or as paving the way for a new transatlantic security arrangement. Whatever happens in Europe, for political and economic reasons the US does not have the option of retreating from European affairs.[4] At the same time, its reservations about the ESDP will continue for some time to come.[5]

As most Western European states are members of both NATO and the EU (giving these states a *de facto* 'double veto'), they can remain Atlanticists while also being staunchly European.[6] This initially unsettled and puzzled the US.[7] As Nicole Gnesotto observes, the US has a problem with Europe becoming too parasitic, and also with it becoming too equal.[8] It is a matter of perspective whether the US or the Europeans have most at stake in NATO.[9]

Nonetheless, the EU and the US seem to have reached a new level in their relations. The change comes from two directions. The first is the fact that the ESDP has fundamentally altered the institutional setting, and the shape of the transatlantic link. The second is that it suits the US for the Europeans to take increasing responsibility for their own security, while the US focuses on new priorities such as homeland defence.[10] This does not mean that the US does not care about Europe, that NATO is obsolete or that transatlantic ties are cut. But it does signal a new transatlantic relationship, where the US and Europe cooperate foremost on a global level, fighting common threats and defending common interests. The ESDP and the US focuses on homeland defence are not about strategic disengagement, nor are they a question of choosing between NATO and the ESDP. Rather, they mean developing new relations outside of the traditional transatlantic link, based on trade, shared strategic interests and common objectives in conflict prevention and stability.

Arguably, the autonomous decision-making capabilities that the EU is developing are no more dramatic or damaging to NATO than US decision-making autonomy. EU autonomy will make the

European pillar within NATO stronger, and autonomy is a normal part of a strategic partnership of equals. In reality, Europe will not stand alone any more than the US will, and cooperation will thrive as long as it benefits both partners. Almost nobody wants NATO to dissolve, and almost all the European states genuinely want a strong alliance, a strong CFSP/ESDP and healthy links with the US. Squaring this circle will at times be challenging, but far from impossible. There are some real differences, over trade, multilateralism, arms control, the role of the UN, the pre-emptive use of force, the death penalty, or multilateral initiatives such as the Kyoto Protocol or the International Criminal Court (ICC). The challenge lies in managing these disputes without allowing individual issues to taint the core of cooperative responsibilities and shared interests.

One of the key challenges concerns how the US perceives burden-sharing. The ESDP represents a new form of burden-sharing, rendering the traditional debate on this question obsolete.[11] The US has traditionally focused on persuading the Europeans to increase their defence spending and fulfil the DCI, rather than encouraging restructuring, reform or multinational coordination.[12] In 2001, the US DoD argued that 'unresponsive defense budgets pose a risk of stagnating or, even worse, eroding Alliance capabilities'.[13] This exemplifies the generally narrow perspective on this question in the US.[14] If the US continues to measure burden-sharing by the standards of European defence budgets, the DCI, alignment with JV 2010/2020, a US-defined RMA/transformation or Congressional demands, transatlantic squabbling will continue.

In place of traditional aspects of security and defence, tomorrow's strategic partnership should, and probably will, be dominated by trade, international politics, global crisis management, safeguarding common interests and commodities, arms control, non-proliferation and export-control regimes, counter-terrorism, international crime and strategic defences.[15] Traditional military capabilities will play a minor role.[16] The NATO-centric view is no longer relevant, and it will be in Washington's interests to have a broader and more multifaceted perception of, and relationship with, the ESDP, CFSP and European security arrangements. For all elements but European collective defence and high-end peace enforcement in Europe, the EU will be a more interesting partner in global crisis management than the European pillar within NATO. The new transatlantic strategic partnership will be a blend of respect, prestige, competition and cooperation in almost all fields. Developing this new partnership will not resolve the debates on European priorities, procurement budgets, NATO–EU relations and how best to address global threats – but these questions will be dealt with differently, and hopefully in a more constructive way.

For some time to come, the EU will remain a union of independent states, with their own interests and priorities.[17] Europe wants to be treated as the equal of the US, while maintaining national agendas and close bilateral contacts – which, from an outsider's perspective, is perhaps not a logical position. The challenge is for Europe to take steps towards greater coherence and to prove its worth as a strategic partner in global security. Conversely, it may be in Washington's interest to prove to the EU and the European states that the US provides a multifaceted security-projecting capability, and has more to offer than military might.

The challenges of EU–NATO cooperation

The question is not whether the ESDP should or could replace NATO, but how to bring about effective cooperation and coordination. Both the EU and NATO are mere institutions to enhance their member states' policies and assets, and facilitate cooperation and coordination between members. It is up to the members, particularly the major players with membership in both, to develop sound institutional working relationships.

Although the higher goals of the EU and NATO are the same and their membership broadly similar, there are fundamental differences. Their histories differ, as do their approaches to defence and crisis management, their expertise and their mandates. Other points of difference are size, budget, decision-making processes and command-and-control capabilities. The role of individual states within the two organisations – not least the US – is not equal, nor is the level of national sovereignty.

A strict division of labour between NATO and the EU would not be good for Europe, the US or the institutional development of either organisation. Above all, no European state wants two separate force structures. As the ESDP's formal focus is the Petersberg spectrum, there is a risk that NATO will be relegated to collective defence.[18] The alternative is to accept duplication and to continue to focus on commonalities, coordination and cooperation in military crisis management.[19] Even in the longer term, duplication will be good for NATO's vitality, European capabilities and the transatlantic strategic partnership as a whole.

NATO's status as the sole Western security structure has fundamentally changed with the ESDP, and it is probable, as Stephen Walt argued back in 1998, that the high-water mark of transatlantic security cooperation has passed. Transatlantic security cooperation has entered a new phase.[20] NATO's comparative advantages include the direct involvement of the US in European defence through US security guarantees to its allies; its role as a security forum and a forum for interoperability and common military standards; access to US force transformation; and its function as a structure to provide transatlantic cooperation in times of need. The pan-European nature of NATO and its partnerships, the stabilising effect it has had on Central and South-Eastern Europe and its role in European crisis management since 1992 are all valuable for European security. NATO will remain an important organisation and will retain its relevance, even in a transformed strategic partnership. Relations between the EU and NATO should be developed as long as NATO continues to play an important role in security and the EU–US relationship is embryonic, and until such time as the EU has addressed key flaws in its crisis-management capabilities and ended its dependence on US assets and capabilities for high-end military operations.

Chapter 4

Europe's Operational Limitations

On the basis of existing capability initiatives, the planned development of EU crisis-management capabilities and an evolving EU–US strategic partnership, this chapter assesses what an autonomous EU will be able to do, in strategic and operational terms, in 2003 and at the end of the decade – and what it will not be able to do. It analyses the EU's dependence on NATO and the US, and looks at the question of EU intelligence capabilities.

What an autonomous EU can and cannot do in the military field

Western Europe can cope with almost any crisis and war, including the situations envisaged in the three scenarios outlined in Chapter 2. But this is only possible if Europe is prepared to accept higher risks for engaged forces, if speed is not critical and if there are no competing military priorities. If Western European states can accept casualties and collateral damage, and if there is time to build political consensus and to deploy forces, then Europe can do a great deal on its own. However, if US high-intensity warfare is the only standard, if risks have to be kept to a minimum and a high operational tempo is needed to maintain public support and political alliances, then Europe faces major challenges in the next decade. On the other hand, Europeans and Americans have different global ambitions and priorities, and it is probable that the EU's standard of intervention will differ from the standards expected of NATO or a US-led coalition.

Although the development of the EU's capabilities since late 1999 has been vulnerable to criticism, not least because the political nature of the effort has been so dominant, the ESDP's structures and processes have taken huge strides forward, in a very short time, in terms of qualitative and quantitative output. The integrity, professionalism and initiative of the officers and civil servants involved, and the momentum of the ESDP process, should not be underestimated. Even a decrease in top-level political interest in the ESDP and the absence of spectacular new initiatives would therefore not mean that European integration and coordination in the security field had come to a halt. On the contrary, without a phase of consolidation after such an intense period of political initiatives, the whole ESDP enterprise would risk becoming a mere flow of announcements without much implementation and substance.

Military capabilities on the drawing board or in the pipeline

Half of European NATO members increased their defence spending in real terms, albeit marginally, in 2000. Elements such as intelligence received a boost due to the war on terrorism. Nevertheless, European defence budgets are unlikely to increase significantly in the medium term. On the contrary, the overall trend in total European defence spending remains downward in real terms. In addition, the challenges of multinational coordination and procurement will not disappear, and the restructuring needed for substantial savings and for the reorientation of many European armed forces will remain difficult. Conversely, the cuts in European defence expenditure throughout much of the 1990s have obviously not been severe enough to force governments into far-reaching multinational cooperation, the pooling of assets and capabilities, role specialisation or the fundamental rationalisation of defence industries.[1]

Relatively little money is spent on force transformation, procurement and research and development. While the UK and Sweden spend more than a third of their defence budgets in these areas, and France more than a quarter, the majority of Western European countries spend less than 20%.[2] Nonetheless, a number of large procurement projects with considerable defence-industrial potential are in the pipeline. Europeans have committed themselves to producing and procuring approximately 180 Airbus A400M strategic-lift aircraft. Even if this figure is not fully attained, there will probably be a significant and specific capability increase (though it will not give the Europeans a truly heavy-load, long-distance airlift capability because the A400M carries only 50% more than the common C-130 and a fraction of the C-17 or C-5).[3] The increased coordination and pooling of existing sea and airlift, fighters and aircraft logistics could enhance overall European lift capability. However, a German proposal for a joint European air-transport command, launched in the wake of the Kosovo campaign and included as a goal in the DCI, has not made progress.[4] The idea is rational, cost-effective and technically simple, but obviously unpopular in European capitals. Perhaps the Prague Capabilities Commitment will help European governments change their minds. France and the UK are acquiring several types of cruise missile, and the French and Germans are developing reconnaissance satellites (*Helios II* and *SARLupe*). Several states are acquiring UAVs and advanced fighters (*Rafale*, *Eurofighter* and *Gripen*), enhancing their precision-strike capability and acquiring new tactical communications systems, the *Meteor* air-to-air missile, *Patriot* PAC-3 extended-air-defence systems, main battle tanks, tactical airlift (C-130Js, C-295s), theatre transport such as the NH-90 helicopter, amphibious-warfare ships (LPD and ALSL) and roll-on/roll-off sealift.

Many of the DCI 'wish-list' items are not given the same priority as these projects. In fact, some take up such a large portion of procurement budgets in certain countries that new programmes more in tune with the network-centric philosophy of the DCI cannot gain ground. It remains unlikely that NATO members will jointly acquire airborne ground-surveillance systems (Joint-STARS-type assets) or new early-warning systems such as AWACS in the medium term. Other challenges or capability gaps identified in the DCI include plans for an integrated interoperable logistics information architecture, multinational exercise programmes, operational simulation devices, full interoperability between tactical communications systems, airfield-management systems, advanced air defence, combat search-and-rescue, air-to-air refuelling, electronic counter-measures/jamming aircraft, defences against weapons of mass destruction and their means of delivery and protection against modern sea mines and torpedoes. Europe is still a long way from even contemplating moving communications, including satellite communication, to broadband capabilities, an element given high priority by the US DoD and the very essence of US military transformation. For both the US and Europe, it is not a question of physics and know-how but of investment priorities and vision. As of 2002, it looked unlikely that any European government would be prepared to scrap a major equipment project such as a new line of fighters, battle tanks or helicopters in favour of something as low profile as communications, regardless of the revolutionary potential.

In the area of NBC protection, not least in the light of terrorist threats, there are acute needs in personal equipment and in safeguarding both military and non-military infrastructure within the area of operations and at home. Further capability gaps identified in the HPC – particularly in support, logistics, engineering and medical capabilities – are equally vital in crisis-management operations. Advanced fighter aircraft, precision-guided munitions, non-lethal weapons, SEAD and day/night and all-weather air-weapon systems are all being developed, but not in sufficient numbers to significantly enhance Europe's autonomous military capabilities.[5] Moreover, the proportion of logistics and support units made available to the full range of NATO missions has not, and probably will not, increase significantly.

Many current European procurement projects constitute massive duplication on a European scale. Is it wise of Europe to develop so many different types of traditional capabilities, such as main battle tanks, infantry fighting vehicles, fighters, submarines and surface combatants? For tomorrow's challenges, does Europe really need these platforms, none of which are categorised by any of the WEU, NATO or the EU capability inventories as shortfalls?

Even if projects on the drawing board are funded (which is far from certain), it will take time for new assets to become operational capabilities. In the case of the A400M, the first aircraft will fly in 2008 at the earliest, but realistically probably later. It will be several more years before units are fully operational, and a sufficient number of aircraft exists to make a significant contribution to Europe's overall airlift capability. In the meantime, leasing US C-17s like the UK has done may be an option, if strategic airlift is being acquired for operational, rather than mainly defence-industrial, reasons. For other major procurement programmes, such as reconnaissance satellites, cruise missiles, tactical airlift and advanced fighters, quantities are relatively small, and there will be little operational impact until 2005–2010. [6] It is also questionable whether sufficient money will be spent on the less spectacular capability gaps identified by the DCI and in the HPC. High-profile pet projects with greater defence-industrial links or clear application to defending against terrorism (of which there are few in the area of conventional military procurement) may attract the lion's share of political attention in European capitals whether they are needed (from a European perspective) or not. Realistically, based on what is in the pipeline and even taking the Prague Capabilities Commitment into account, a substantial increase in Europe's overall capability to successfully engage in high-end crisis management should not be expected in the medium term.

Many allies have indicated through their commitments to DCI-related Force Goals that they are not taking DCI implementation seriously.[7] As the US DoD noted in a report to Congress in March 2001, in many respects progress towards DCI objectives has been disappointingly slow.[8] The fact that the US had to relaunch a slimmed-down capability initiative in preparation for NATO's 2002 Prague Summit is further proof of the lack of progress – at least from the US perspective and by the standards of US military transformation. The DCI capability gaps will limit the EU's capacity to engage in the most demanding Petersberg tasks, not to mention US-led coalitions. These gaps will be particularly evident should the EU choose to engage autonomously.

Equally, it is questionable whether the HPC and ECAP will make much difference. It could be argued that a considerable portion of European force modernisation would probably have happened anyway – even without the DCI and the Headline Goal. The continued investment by European governments in traditional capabilities indicates that the capability initiatives have either not been understood, or have had little or no impact on procurement priorities. Perhaps the greatest benefits of these capability initiatives are political; their 'added value' may only develop in the longer term through increasingly coordinated defence planning and the development of new capabilities for a wider spectrum of engagement.

It is also questionable whether the projects planned by Europe's defence industry are on the same technological and interoperability level as the US. US capabilities are often a generation ahead of the Europeans doctrinally and technically, which means that interoperability is likely to remain a problem.[9] The speed of the US military transformation process paves the way for even greater capability gaps. However, just as it is important for the Europeans to be interoperable with the US, so too the US must secure interoperability with the Europeans, if it wants to work in coalitions and cooperate within the NATO framework.[10] Joint and combined US and European rapid reaction forces such as the NRF could be a step in the right direction.

The EU's military operational limit in 2003

In military terms, what is Europe able to manage on its own in 2003? For corps-sized operations, the European Military Staff as currently envisaged will probably be too small for effective operational planning (although this is a view not shared by all in the EU Military Staff as it grows larger and more confident – even in the planning sphere). In times of crisis, it is likely that planning will be supported (or essentially executed) by a lead nation or lead planning headquarters, identified early on. There is no reason to doubt that the British, French and German joint operational staff could produce credible plans, ideally (but not necessarily) in coordination with, and/or with the support of, NATO operational planning staff.

The primary constraint would be the time allotted to producing the palette required, from pre-crisis contingency plans to concepts of operation and operational plans, plus the time needed for them to be cleared by all the involved structures and member states. There is a risk that the lack of linkage between member states, the ESDP structures and operational staff (and back up the chain of command) will prove a bottleneck in a crisis. There is significant political sensitivity around establishing 'EU-only' structures and processes, and creating multinational staff out of national operational staff, along with secure command, control, communications, computer and intelligence links between all the levels and parties involved, is a costly and complex process. In the meantime, either multinationality and/or effective and secure links will probably have to be sacrificed. Transmitting secure broadband data from surveillance and reconnaissance assets across national contingents is an even more distant possibility.

In terms of actual operational capability, the forces committed to the Headline Goal do not constitute a fighting force, but rather are a mere catalogue of capabilities committed on a case-by-case basis by individual states. Nevertheless, the sum of just the German, British, French, Italian and Spanish contributions represents a sizeable capability of over 60,000 soldiers and almost 300 combat aircraft for a continuous one-year operation. Europe can handle a situation like *Operation Alba*: a brigade-sized multinational operation, where combat intensity is relatively low and there is no organised resistance and therefore little need for advanced air and naval support. Logistical trails are short, and the small force can be managed even without a large logistics base or host-nation support and infrastructure. However, even in *Operation Alba* Europe had no capacity to escalate. In fact, the Combined Joint Planning Staff in NATO had prepared a contingency plan for a US-led evacuation should the need arise.[11] In 2002, while the EU was politically prepared to take over from NATO's European-led operation *Amber Fox* in Macedonia, some member states were reluctant to do so for fear of over-stretching their forces because of other peace-support commitments.

Even without external help, the 'Assistance to Civilians' scenario, including smaller evacuation operations, should not pose a major challenge for the EU. The UK, France, Spain, Italy and the Netherlands have long had such a capability and EU coordination should be manageable – particularly if there are one or two lead nations. In an acute evacuation scenario, it is also probable that the luxury of EU multinationality can be sacrificed. The 'Conflict Prevention/Preventive Deployment' scenario is also within current European capacities, though there would be some flaws in the high-end spectrum. These could perhaps be managed on a bilateral basis, or with a marginally higher tolerance for collateral damage and risk. Gradual improvements in sustainability mean that a one-year operation of up to 60,000 troops for the Conflict Prevention/Preventive Deployment scenario is not a major issue. Unless the EU merely takes over an already-established mission, the main challenges will lie in drawing down existing deployments and reducing redeployment time. Should forces need new training and equipment, or if the deployment takes place in difficult climates, sustainability could become a problem, even for the Conflict Prevention/Preventive Deployment scenario. Concurrent operations would also present problems. Certain combinations of operations, particularly taking place a good distance apart, would put greater strains on some capabilities than would be the case were the most demanding scenario occurring alone.

Strategic decision-making, operational command and control and intelligence will remain bottlenecks. Indeed, the whole process of EU decision-making and unity of command will remain underdeveloped. In intelligence, even with rapid development, French and German reconnaissance satellites will be operational at the earliest in 2004, and European sensors will remain few in number and, in most cases, at least a generation behind American assets. Intelligence cooperation among EU members and the EU's central assessment capability will remain poor. On the hardware side, Europe's ability to act autonomously in high-tempo peace-enforcement operations and its high-end projection capabilities will remain limited. Perhaps the most dangerous limitation will be Europe's poor capacity to escalate. Europe will not have additional combat-ready divisions, carrier battle groups and marine and air expeditionary forces deployable at short notice, either for escalation or for large-scale evacuations; nor will it have the means to deploy and support them.

EU members will be able to do much in military crisis management by 2003. But autonomous, high-tempo peace enforcement in a non-permissive environment will not be possible – particularly if the operation is larger than divisional, risks have to be kept low and deployment times within the Headline Goal criteria. At the high end of the spectrum, EU states will remain dependent on the US for operational, and perhaps also for political, support.

The EU's military operational limit in 2010

On the basis of what has been decided as of late 2002, significant increases in European military crisis-management capabilities are likely by 2010 – at least by European standards, as defined in 1999–2002 – even if the ESDP process slows down. It is probable that both sea and airlift will increase, although whether they do so on the scale envisaged at the beginning of the decade is less clear. Nevertheless, mobility and readiness will improve. Precision-guided munitions and cruise missiles will be more readily available, and electronic-warfare and SEAD capabilities will probably also have increased. It is, however, difficult to see significant improvements in operational command-and-control networks and support elements, including logistics, engineering and medical support.

By 2010, military reform will have been completed in France, and probably also in Germany. Most European armed forces will be geared towards military crisis management, and expeditionary capabilities will play a central role. Multinationality and interoperability will probably have further evolved. Sustainability, deployability and effective engagement will have moved forward. The EU structures, and probably also individual member states, will probably be better at strategic decision-making, intelligence-gathering and strategic (and perhaps operational) planning than they were at the beginning of the decade. By 2010, it is likely that EU states will be able to meet the 2003 Headline Goal in full. This does not, however, mean that Europe will have fulfilled every DCI objective or that the capability gap across the Atlantic will have decreased. On the contrary; the US will have made its own capability increases, particularly in high-technology areas such as command, control and communications and in the whole sphere of sensors and intelligence gathering and dissemination. Judging by the much larger investment being made in the US on network-centric warfare elements, the technical gap is bound to increase. The question is whether the doctrinal and operational gap will be even greater.

Much will depend on the level of US–European cooperation in combined experimentation and force development.

Defence planning

EU defence planning, particularly if non-military and military capabilities are linked, can play an important role in increasing European capabilities. The EU Capabilities Development Mechanism will probably be geared not only to updating commitments and filling gaps, but also to formulating political goals, setting operational targets, managing national commitments and future capabilities enhancements, linking lessons learnt to planned needs and introducing peer pressure to the review phase. Key aspects are the implementation of crisis-management mechanisms and capabilities, the quality validation of those mechanisms and capabilities, and the establishment of truly operational capabilities for joint and multinational war-fighting.

However, by 2010 the Headline Goal is bound to have changed in line with changes in EU cohesion, integration and perceived threats. Where yesterday's goals are directed towards conventional military crisis management, tomorrow's may focus on other challenges, ranging from territorial defence and counter-terrorism to cyber-attacks and CBRNE weapons. The EU's goals may develop along the lines of its comparative advantages, and non-military crisis management and conflict prevention may be seen as more important than the military components.

Beyond 2010, European processes, procedures, doctrines and modes of operation may have developed in such a way that they do not fully correlate to US and NATO standards, although a certain level of interoperability would most likely be maintained. In the longer term, depending on the involvement of the UK in the development of the EU's operational capability and cooperation between Germany, France, Italy and the Benelux countries, it should not be taken for granted that Anglo-Saxon methods and procedures will remain the natural choice in all areas of European cooperation. There is thus a risk that this may add to further interoperability challenges with the US.

Legal and political considerations

The EU sees itself as a sophisticated international player with high moral standards and values. As a result, a number of factors could limit its operational capability. Although the Headline Goal is not bound by a formal UN mandate, high standards will be set for EU intervention.[12] The intervention must be 'just', a concept which, aside from self-defence, has historically included punishing an aggressor or intervening on behalf of victims of aggression.[13] The intervention must be morally justified and must be a last resort, to be used only when diplomatic and non-violent means have failed. Thus, few EU military crisis-management engagements will be initiated without considerable international debate and the lengthy exploration of non-violent alternatives. Surprise and pre-emptive force are unlikely.

Given the heterogeneous nature of the EU's composition, the fact that many member states would want a UN mandate before any military intervention and the need for close consultation with NATO, there is little reason to believe that securing legal justification for action will be any quicker in the EU than it is in UN peace-support operations – unless clear interests are threatened, as was the case with *Operation Alba* in 1997 or after the terrorist strikes in the US in 2001. (Less adversarial forms of military crisis management, such as naval patrols, as well as operations in response to acute situations, such as evacuations, can of course be performed nationally, or collectively under the EU, without any formal mandate or lengthy debate.) There may also be competition between the EU and NATO. EU bilateral dialogue with all NATO member states and Russia, and perhaps coordination and cooperation, is another potentially complicating factor – particularly if key players want to delay an operation, or prefer a different institutional slant.

Two further factors may also be important. The first is proportionality, which demands certain capabilities, like detailed intelligence and precision-guided munitions. 'Dumb bombs' are not politically acceptable unless vital or existential interests are at stake.[14] Second, there must be a reasonable chance of success (and again raises the issue of escalation). The need to define proportionality throughout a crisis, and with it to set targeting criteria and operational tempos, together with continuous assessment of the likelihood of success, could lead to debate among EU members.

Target selection by consensus does not sound easy, or militarily decisive. As long as all EU states must give their consent to military action under an EU flag, decision-making is likely to be complicated.

Before leaving his post in mid-2000, SACEUR Wesley Clark suggested that the gradualist approach to combat that NATO had demonstrated over Kosovo might not succeed the next time the alliance used force.[15] If NATO (with the full support and dominance of the US) tends to behave this way, how cohesive and decisive can the EU hope to be in crisis management? For operations or threats that demand a more proactive or pre-emptive approach, or where speed is important, national intervention by one or more allies or other *ad hoc* arrangements under a lead nation might be more appropriate, with or without a symbolic blessing from the EU and/or NATO member states. If vital interests are at stake or if a broadly-recognised case could be made for self-defence, NATO or a coalition of the willing with NATO's political support will for the foreseeable future remain the natural choice.

Europe's intelligence capability

Whatever CFSP or ESDP activity takes place, be it in the pre-crisis or the crisis phase, intelligence for strategic decision-making is paramount. Along with operational self-sustainability, autonomous decision-making is a formal EU goal. Whether an engagement demands EU–NATO and EU–US coordination, or if it is an autonomous EU operation, EU bodies and member states must be capable of taking decisions based on their own assessments. Given that intelligence cooperation in NATO has been non-existent, why should cooperation be any more effective within the EU? The difference is that the autonomous strategic decision-making capability is already a political goal; in the near future, there will be a political and operational demand for EU intelligence.

There are two purposes for EU intelligence. The first relates to long-term conflict prevention and the EU's position as an international actor. Pre-crisis intelligence can help the EU to use its economic, diplomatic and military conflict-prevention means more effectively. The second intelligence element is related to operational engagement in times of crisis. Although each demands very different kinds of analysis and capabilities, both are essential for strategic decision-making.

Current processes are not satisfactory because they are based on the principle that all intelligence, with the exception of the EU's Satellite Centre, is channelled from member states; the ESDP structures, including the Joint Situation Centre, should be happy with whatever they get. As a consequence, the EU's assessment capability is confined to a tiny Joint Situation Centre in Brussels, and there is little capacity either to check the validity of national intelligence or to compile broader intelligence assessments where national military intelligence is only one part of the equation. Little national intelligence is tailored to the needs of the ESDP structures, or put in the CFSP and ESDP context. For quick and effective strategic decision-making, current processes are not good enough.

A comprehensive joint European intelligence-assessment capability could prove an invaluable step towards more effective EU strategic decision-making for both conflict prevention and crisis management. Such an intelligence capability, within the intergovernmental Second Pillar of the EU, could also function as an intelligence coordinator in fields such as terrorism and unconventional threats. In the HHC of 2000, EU states identified the need for a facility for intelligence fusion, analysis, storage and dissemination, and for an EU Military Staff Intelligence Division.[16] Although the latter already exists, it falls short of the comprehensive intelligence function required by the EU.[17] Equally, the SG/HR Policy Unit, albeit highly capable, is too small and not geared towards intelligence analysis or coordination. The Policy Unit would be better able to serve the SG/HR and the Political and Security Committee with assessments and option proposals if it were supported by an intelligence-analysis capability. Other functions, such as the Director-General for External Affairs (primarily DGE VIII), would also benefit.

The EU's envisaged intelligence function would provide common assessments of political and operational relevance. Although any structure would spend much time comparing and compiling national assessments, the function would have to be able to produce its own analyses and assessments, both short- and long-term. This would demand a sizeable capability. EU member states would not only have full access to EU assessments, but would also be obliged to contribute raw and processed data. The intelligence function would be one element in an over-arching European network of bilateral and multilateral intelligence cooperation.

Using capabilities that already exist, the Satellite Centre could become the hub for the interpretation of satellite intelligence and imagery from European commercial and military assets. The key for the EU, via the centre, is to have increased access to French and German military satellites, including in some cases resolution codes and algorithms. For this to be a European project, full access should be provided to all EU member states, unless they choose to opt out. Sharing operating costs, and perhaps research and development costs, would have to be agreed between all the states that would benefit from the imagery, or that are involved in the EU intelligence function.

EU intelligence cooperation should also be developed at the tactical level. Experience from peace-support operations in the Balkans shows that, although intelligence remains a jealously-guarded national commodity, tactical-level cooperation is possible. The National Intelligence Cell network in SFOR and KFOR headquarters is a useful and proven model for EU-led peace-support operations.

In terms of data input, most capability assessments stress the need for high-end technical platforms such as satellites. Although defence-industrial interests, technology transfer and national prestige are significant issues, it is important to recognise that expensive platforms are no panacea.[18] High-tech assets might be spectacular and costly, but they are relatively useless unless the data they produce are properly received, assessed, contextualised and disseminated to the relevant bodies or individuals – and all in time to be useful. Real-time intelligence calls for huge resources in order to direct the satellites, receive the data, interpret them and forward them to the relevant platform or decision-maker. The ESDP structures will not have the capacity for quick interpretation, dissemination and input to policy channels in the short to medium term, let alone a real-time capability. Furthermore, for decent coverage, several different types and more than a handful of satellites are needed; however, their provision is unlikely within the next decade. Besides, almost all threat/intelligence assessments need to be based on multiple sources – not just technical data.

On the other hand, if the main function of the satellites is to give sporadic input on global flashpoints, or to provide Europe with collateral information against which to verify US intelligence, Europe could probably manage with a handful of French and German military satellites. With clear commitment and financing, such a capability could be realised in the medium term, perhaps by 2005. This would still be a clear case of duplication, just as for most military assets that exist on both sides of the Atlantic. Such a limited European capability would not make the EU self-sufficient in intelligence (as called for in the Headline Goal), and the EU and its members would still remain largely dependent on US intelligence capabilities.[19]

As well as developing satellites for a limited autonomous capability, there must also be operational alternatives. Much can be done through modifying existing platforms, using the whole palette of intelligence sources and through international coordination and cooperation. Europe's wide array of signals and human intelligence, coupled with existing satellite and air assets, could provide much strategic and operational intelligence for conflict prevention and crisis management if cooperation increased. For these combined assets to be effective, they must be coordinated at the strategic EU level, and fully integrated at the operational level.

Operationally, a combination of top-end special forces (such as the UK's Special Air Service (SAS) or France's Commando Parachute Group), advanced signals-intelligence capabilities (such as those provided by Sweden in Bosnia and Kosovo), UAVs and aerial photo and radar reconnaissance can, in most operational situations, provide more relevant intelligence at a fraction of the investment and operating cost than satellite imagery and US Joint-STAR input.

Challenges for EU conflict prevention and crisis management

The two greatest threats facing the ESDP are failure to act successfully and disengagement by a key European player. In the pre-crisis phase, Europeans are likely to have trouble deciding if a crisis is developing, what sort of crisis it is and how best to deal with it. National policies, prestige and ambition may collide, and nationally-slanted intelligence may further diminish the chances of achieving a common view. Atlanticists would probably disagree with advocates of a European approach, while others would perhaps opt out altogether. As long as vital interests are not at stake, issues of internal EU and US–EU coordination and links to multilateral bodies like the UN and the Organisation for Security and Cooperation in Europe (OSCE) would probably further complicate decision-making. Economic, diplomatic and military instruments may not be properly coordinated or used to their full potential.

Should the EU decide to mount a military operation, this would obviously mean that conflict prevention had failed. Even with a military operation under way (with at least the political support of all member states), any perceived shortcomings would damage the credibility of the EU and the ESDP. Challenges would include ensuring political cohesion among the members and other contributors, making sure that strategic decision-making did not falter and coping with military capability flaws and poor means of military escalation. The US could also choose not to support the operation – even if asked to do so; however, any perceived lack of support would affect NATO solidarity. A divided and frustrated Europe will not produce a stronger alliance or a credible strategic partner for the US.

On the other hand, even a perceived operational failure, or an embarrassing bail-out by the US or NATO, would probably not halt the CFSP or ESDP. Finger-pointing would temporarily damage European cohesion and leave a bitter after-taste, but the CFSP and ESDP are much larger phenomena than a one-off military operation. As Alyson Bailes argues, greater operational experience will make the CFSP more 'street-wise' and effective. Engagement will gradually increase the level of non-military and military coordination, and will enhance EU effectiveness. It is probable that the EU will also learn lessons from, and be influenced by, non-EU engagements.

Should decision-making at the EU level prove impossible for a prolonged period, perhaps several years, or if a series of crisis-management efforts are seen as failures, alternatives to the CFSP and ESDP may well develop. There will always be European states willing to cooperate outside international organisations, if these bodies are not functioning adequately. On the other hand, even if institutional cooperation succeeds but the mission fails – based on the experience of UN and NATO operations – the EU as an institution will probably be a useful scapegoat.

The second threat – disengagement by one of the key European players – would potentially have more serious and longer-term consequences than failure. Should the UK, France or Germany turn their back on the common EU foreign and defence policy or actively obstruct the EU, the ESDP project would swiftly stall.[20] Any long-term stagnation would be damaging for European integration as a whole and for relations among European states, particularly if the US at the same time gave priority to homeland defence, leaving Europe fragmented and lonely, and without the ability to act as a strategic partner with Washington. Large-scale recession, a collapse in the value of the euro or mass unemployment could quickly shift political attention away from secondary issues like the ESDP. Such serious developments could affect defence budgets, capability-building and most aspects of crisis management. Policies may turn inwards, towards protectionism and re-nationalisation. In the words of Helmut Schmidt, the EU is still a very young and fragile creature, and can be destroyed by national egotism as well as by international upheavals.[21]

Until effective European strategic decision-making structures are in place, and until the EU can effectively coordinate economic, diplomatic and military elements, Europe as a coherent defence entity will carry little weight or credibility, its operational limitations evident for all to see. As of late 2003, and with the Headline Goal deadline, the ESDP will be fair game for international criticism. The EU will have functioning structures at the higher level and a considerable number of capabilities in place, but they will not be fully efficient, effective or potent in conflict prevention and crisis management.

This vulnerability cannot be blamed on NATO, on the US or on new threats. The US and NATO have offered their support and cooperation. Although close cooperation is rational and logical, the US or NATO as an institution cannot enhance the EU's crisis-management capabilities, military, non-military or bureau-cratic. It is up to the Europeans, and above all the UK, France and Germany, to rationalise, coordinate, cooperate and produce better capabilities. Only by increasing its capabilities by innovative and proactive measures can Europe reduce its vulnerability and lay the foundations for credible crisis management.

Chapter 5

Practical Steps To Increase European Capabilities

The prospects for increasing European capabilities for conflict prevention and the management of international crises are good. The question is how significant the increase will be, in what time-frame it will be effected and which focus further capability initiatives will have.

Despite good intentions and a legion of NATO and EU military capability initiatives, progress is slow. Over the next five years or so, it is unlikely that the increase in capabilities will be anything more than marginal. It takes time to build platforms and equipment, to train personnel and to build a military capability – regardless of increases in defence expenditure. Only marginal capability increases are in the procurement pipeline, and a significant increase in Europe's defence expenditure is not feasible under current political conditions. On the contrary, defence expenditure will continue to decrease in many European states. For many voters and governments, it makes sense to take money away from defence and spend it on the police (for counter-terrorism and international operations), foreign aid, domestic civil protection against natural disasters, or even healthcare. The opportunities for greater and more relevant output lie in the field of national reprioritisation and European coordination.

The sum of the capabilities committed to the Headline Goal catalogue is substantial, and Europe will be able to do much on its own. However, because member states lack a handful of capabilities they say they need for the most demanding or geographically distant scenarios, the full Headline Goal ambitions will not be met by late 2003, or indeed for much of the decade. On the other hand, EU members have set their own goals, interpreted them and developed scenarios, and then identified which assets and capabilities would be needed to meet the most challenging situations. The flaws in military capabilities add an incentive for national defence procurement – particularly for those EU member states that have retained major defence-industrial capacities.

The outlook is more promising for the non-military elements of crisis management. Given the EU's low starting point, any increase is bound to be significant. The potential for development in this field is huge. The EU's goals, ranging from police capacity and state-building to civil protection and elements of conflict prevention, will probably be met by late 2003.

These outcomes are not, however, pre-determined, and Europe could substantially increase its capacities even in the medium term, and could do so at little expense. The greatest potential for significantly increasing Europe's capabilities lies in the following areas: enhanced strategic decision-making; intelligence coordination; the development of Europe's conventional military capabilities through increased coordination; national and functional coordination within the Union; and pragmatic EU–NATO and EU–US cooperation.

Enhancing European strategic decision-making

The EU's conflict-prevention and crisis-management capabilities would be significantly increased if its strategic decision-making were enhanced. To achieve this calls for centralised EU coordination of the economic, diplomatic and military and non-military elements of conflict prevention and crisis management, and a single European voice. Realistically, there will not be a common foreign and security policy on every issue in international relations, but there may be room for a common European approach in many, if not most, cases. Even so, centralised EU coordination will not and cannot replace bilateral ties between states within the EU, and across the Atlantic. Strategic EU coordination would be a complement, but not a substitute, for existing ties.

Ideally, one body should coordinate all elements of the ESDP and external relations with states and regions in potential areas of crisis. Only when trade, diplomatic initiatives, loan policies, national and EU threat-reduction schemes, national NGO initiatives and regional relations and crisis-management tools are dynamically linked can conflict prevention be successful – whatever the challenge. Furthermore, this body should coordinate crisis management and intelligence, including monitoring potential and ongoing crises, bilateral military cooperation, non-proliferation, counter-terrorism and arms and technology transfers. Such a body must grasp long-term capability development, defence-industrial cooperation and policy coordination and development within the EU. Only when these elements are tied together can the EU's capability in conflict prevention and crisis management reach its full potential.

Enhanced strategic decision-making is not just needed in times of crisis. Coordination should be the day-to-day norm in order to contribute to stability projection in the pre-crisis phase. There is much to recommend the Political and Security Committee, complemented by relevant Commission and Third Pillar representatives, as this key coordination structure – a European Security Council with joint national and functional representation. (The actual name of this council is not important, but the function is.) The SG/HR, representing competence and continuity, would be a natural chair for such a body.[1] The challenge is to secure the support of the Commission and the SG/HR and General Secretariat of the Council, and to persuade national capitals, particularly London, Paris and Berlin, to hand such an important task to a body in distant Brussels.

A wider body than the current Political and Security Committee is needed because many of the threats and challenges that the EU will face will demand the involvement of the Commission and the EU's legal/police elements. Effective counter-terrorism demands that policies relating to border control are linked with police coordination. At the same time, trade, loans and sanctions can encourage third countries to cooperate. These efforts may be coupled with military threat assessments from the General Secretariat of the Council and member states, and with military and civilian crisis-management elements that deal with terrorism outside the EU. Regional instability in the Middle East or North Africa, for instance, would call for sophisticated and complex management, using all conflict-prevention and crisis-management elements at the disposal of the EU and its members. One crisis may initially be dealt with in the Second Pillar, and then involve the First and then the Third; another may first involve the Commission, then the CFSP and military and civilian crisis-management elements as it develops.

The boundaries between military and civilian security and internal and external security are more fluid and institutions and states must develop new structures and processes to meet this reality. A joint Security Council where the Political and Security Committee is in the lead and the other two pillars are represented could be a cost-effective, useful instrument for increased security.[2] The only rational alternative to increased coordination across the pillars is to amalgamate the EU pillars altogether.

Practical steps

In terms of the technicalities, the decision-*making* Committee of Permanent Representatives (COREPER) would hand over much of its decision-*shaping* and coordination function in conflict prevention and crisis management to the Political and Security Committee. In the long term, the EU would benefit from having just one body, thus giving a joint cross-pillar Security Council improved decision-making powers. The national representatives on the Political and Security Committee should be given stronger mandates by their governments for quicker decision-making. The question of who is to have what vote in a future EU Security Council is sensitive. The CFSP remains inter-governmental, though a voice, and perhaps a vote, should be given to the other two pillars. The fact that a Security Council would be large, particularly after further EU enlargement, makes consensus-building challenging, and much will depend on the chairman and his staff. On the other hand, the large number of countries represented, plus the weight of the other two pillars, would give the Security Council significant international legitimacy and clout.

The Political and Security Committee will need to develop a more effective support staff. To an extent, such mechanisms and structures already exist in the General Secretariat of the Council, not least in the tiny but important Policy Unit and Joint Situation

Centre. These need to be enhanced, as does the role of the SG/HR. Developing policy input for the Political and Security Committee should be a major focus. The SG/HR and General Secretariat of the Council should produce political contingency plans for all conceivable areas of activity, and should support national representatives on the Political and Security Committee in achieving consensus among member states. Key functions include early warning, situation assessment and strategic planning for medium- to long-term conflict prevention and crisis management, including preventive diplomacy and deployments. The SG/HR and the Political and Security Committee/EU Security Council should spend considerable time looking at latent crises, and challenges that may develop into crises months or years ahead. Long-term conflict prevention is rarely glamorous and always difficult to sell politically, but rational and financially sound. More time and effort should be spent by the Political and Security Committee and the SG/HR (and in the future the proposed EU Security Council) on developing democracy, trade, tolerance and the rule of law, expanding contacts through defence diplomacy and supporting regional security and military cooperation and peacekeeping capabilities in areas of concern beyond the EU.

Expanding international points of contact

The Political and Security Committee and the SG/HR should also broaden their international points of contact. Direct ties through liaison offices and exchanges should be established with major international organisations such as the UN, the OSCE, the World Bank, the International Monetary Fund (IMF) and the International Committee of the Red Cross (ICRC).[3] In principle, these organisations should be informed of all CFSP and ESDP matters, and they should have the opportunity to make contributions.

The relationship between the EU and the US should be given priority, and the input of the US welcomed in matters relating to the CFSP and decision-*shaping* processes. Transatlantic dialogue, including the New Transatlantic Agenda, should be complemented by bilateral ties (liaison personnel and exchanges) with the Political and Security Committee and the SG/HR and staff elements, primarily the Policy Unity, DGE VIII, the Military Staff and the

Military Committee. Although priorities and principles may vary, EU member states should have nothing to hide from the US, and vice-versa. On the contrary, the EU must actively seek coordination and dialogue with the US in all international pre-crisis and crisis matters, ranging from areas of concern and ongoing operations to managing common threats. General coordination of long-term stability projection, plus trade and aid, is particularly important. Again, counter-terrorism and conflict prevention have enormous potential if the EU and the US can develop assessments, share ideas and form compatible policies. Although the US has no formal voice in the EU, just as the EU has none in Washington, ideas should flow freely between them as a matter of course. In addition, EU candidate states and Russia should have liaison officers tied to the General Secretariat of the Council, and via their capitals, and should be invited to contribute ideas and to coordinate with the EU.[4]

This does not mean that the EU should become a chaotic forum in which all international organisations, NGOs and states voice their grievances and concerns, thereby paralysing EU decision-making. But it does mean that the EU CFSP/ESDP structures should listen to other players and, where consistent with the policy of EU members, seek policy coordination and practical cooperation. In practical terms, the Political and Security Committee and the SG/HR could establish hearings and selected working groups in order to channel external input and support coordination.

Initiatives like these call for an enlarged SG/HR Policy Unit, an increased Military and CFSP/ESDP staff and more effective coordination mechanisms with the Commission and national representatives in Brussels. The cost of these enhanced support functions, divided by the number of EU members, is a small price to pay.[5] Establishing these processes can be quickly arranged if there is agreement in London, Paris and Berlin. Although it would take several years before the processes became truly effective, they would significantly increase the EU's capability. The price would lie in loss of national prestige and the option to 'go it alone' – particularly among the more influential EU states.

Establishing EU intelligence coordination
EU intelligence is needed at two levels – the strategic decision-

making level and the operational level – and for two purposes – long-term conflict prevention and active crisis management. In the near future, Europe will need a comprehensive intelligence function for strategic decision-making. With hindsight, such a function could have played an important role in the wake of the September 2001 attacks in the US and the subsequent counter-terrorism campaign. The capability will be paramount in addressing instability and future change in the Middle East. There is a demand for intelligence by the SG/HR (and the Policy Unit), the EU Council (and its Political and Security Committee) and the European Commission. The HHC contains a 'requirement' for an intelligence division under the Military Staff – but this is not of the right calibre.

There is a need for an intelligence unit at the political level, preferably directly under the chairman of the Political and Security Committee and the SG/HR, and closely linked with the Policy Unit.[6] An embryonic capability exists in the Joint Situation Centre, but it is questionable whether this is developing quickly enough, or is sufficiently ambitious. Ideally, the EU intelligence function, in both size and role, should be modelled on the UK's Joint Intelligence Committee.

It is important that EU central intelligence is civilian-led, that it has a multifaceted analysis capability, that it is focused on pre-crisis conflict prevention and has direct access to policy makers. Its task would be to support the ESDP structures and the Political and Security Committee (or a future EU Security Council) in order to increase the coordination and output of the wide palette of EU tools for conflict prevention. Without such an analysis capability the ESDP structures, including the Political and Security Committee, depend on national intelligence assessments alone.

Apart from traditional military intelligence (which should be a minor function), the EU intelligence function would have a wider scope, and include humanitarian, economic and political elements and related assessments, ranging from cyber-threats, terrorism and organised crime to weapons' proliferation. Since risk perceptions differ across the Atlantic, it is important for Europe to produce its own risk assessments.

For both the pre-crisis and crisis phases, input would be channelled via member states' own intelligence and diplomatic services, EU Military Committee representatives and the Satellite Centre. Valuable input pertaining to political, economic, industrial and legal circumstances in states with relations with the EU can also be gleaned from the relevant commission directorates. Open-source intelligence and assessments from independent think-tanks would complement these sources. The key is for the EU to have a sizeable and autonomous analysis body that can produce original and relevant assessments. Security is a concern, but if the top secret standard can be maintained in SHAPE and the NATO Combined Joint Planning Staff, there is no reason why such standards could not be maintained among professionals working with EU intelligence.

The EU intelligence function should also act as a forum for temporary or extraordinary cooperation among national experts. Whether it be a crisis in Macedonia, unrest in a North African state, pre-crisis long-term stability projection or counter-terrorism, national intelligence experts could be pooled at the EU level. These experts should be pre-identified, and should function as informal working groups, together with the EU's permanent intelligence staff. This would allow *ad hoc* intelligence coordination and networking among member states and between national and EU experts, and would also contribute intelligence to the EU national representatives and the ESDP structures.

Increased intelligence coordination is also necessary for reasons of operational safety. Member states' intelligence has to be channelled to the EU during an operation; it would be disastrous if soldiers from a member state were killed, and it later transpired that intelligence which could have avoided the casualties had been withheld by another member state.[7]

As Charles Grant argues, there is no reason why the EU, via an EU intelligence function, could not develop a bilateral relationship with the US.[8] This would make the US feel included, dispel rumours, and pave the way for a flow of intelligence assessments where there are common interests and, at the least, compatible policies. Such cooperation would be a natural part of any strategic partnership.

An EU intelligence function would be rational and potentially highly effective. Much intelligence relating to the Balkans, for instance, is endlessly circulated in European capitals. There is a risk that intelligence coming from the same source (often American) is modified each time it changes hands. The more outdated information becomes, the greater the damage if it proves inaccurate. Today there is massive duplication of European national intelligence capabilities, not least in areas where national interests are less than vital. If the Europeans could share a portion of basic intelligence relating to areas of potential crises, resources could be channelled towards deeper and more focused assessments.

The sensitive issue of intelligence cooperation, the danger of national interpretations and slants, differing national agendas and interests and their effect on national and EU assessments – all will mean that an EU intelligence function, let alone EU–US cooperation, will be challenging. In some ways, a relatively autonomous EU intelligence function under the Political and Security Committee/Security Council will compete with national intelligence services, and the 'ownership' of intelligence and sources could become tricky. Few intelligence services wish to give more attention to European cooperation if this drains resources from their relationship with the US. However, greater openness within an EU framework and increased competition in producing original and relevant data will, in the long term, improve the quality of European intelligence services and European security overall. Meetings among EU member states' directors of military intelligence are a step in the right direction, though the real experts also need to meet and exchange views. It is up to governments to force intelligence services to cooperate and contribute more directly to the CFSP and ESDP.

For an EU intelligence function to be effective and relevant, it would have to have authority, integrity and the respect of the other EU institutions and member states. Its staff would have to be community-funded and recruited directly by the General Secretariat of the Council. Intelligence services would most likely require liaison officers to convey (and translate) sensitive information to those producing the assessments – not dissimilar from the process developed for military intelligence conveyed to the EU Military Staff. To produce new and uniquely relevant intelligence, an EU intelligence body would probably require a minimum of around

100 intelligence experts, excluding national liaison officers and support staff. A clear political directive by EU member states will be vital to the running of the intelligence function, the formulation of intelligence requirements and the national fulfilment of intelligence commitments.

On the hardware side, the EU should also develop its strategic reconnaissance capability. At least a handful of satellites is needed in order to have the ability to verify US intelligence, add a modest autonomous capability and contribute to transatlantic intelligence-gathering in both the conflict-prevention and crisis-management phases. The development of coordinated human intelligence, UAVs, aerial reconnaissance, European air-based ground-surveillance radar, special forces and signals intelligence would give the EU a better operational intelligence capability. Individual EU members and the EU as an institution must have processed and unprocessed intelligence, as well as analysis and assessments, to trade with the US.

Even with the political will to create an EU intelligence function and the establishment of security arrangements, operational cooperation and trust would still take time to develop. Even under favourable conditions, perhaps generated by an acute need for cooperation during a crisis such as the counter-terrorist campaign in 2001 and 2002, it would probably take 5–10 years for EU intelligence coordination to become effective. The development of US–EU cooperation is therefore important, not only for the benefit of European security and the transatlantic link, but also because there is little option in the short to medium term. It is, however, important to note that the development of a relatively autonomous EU intelligence analysis capability is a contribution to transatlantic burden-sharing (both old and new), and does not diminish existing bilateral intelligence cooperation across the Atlantic.

The capability initiatives and the future of European integration

The quest is for greater and more relevant output. The institutional label of the initiatives or forces is less important.

In the military field, it will be important to maintain the momentum of the DCI, the Prague Capabilities Commitment, and the Headline Goal towards deployability, sustainability, effective engagement, survivability, command-and-control systems and interoperability. Whatever the initiative, military forces should become more flexible, potent and better supported for crisis management than they are today. Improvement will not be spectacular or quick, but it will gradually enhance the EU, NATO and the transatlantic strategic partnership. It is also important that Europe acquires the assets and capabilities it needs – not what the US would like Europe to develop. European taxpayers and governments alone decide what is value for money.

The greatest 'new' output will come from those countries that have so far failed to move beyond the old concept of stationary territorial defence, and from those countries that have yet to form deployable, effective and sustainable capabilities for crisis-management operations. Forces must have dual roles [EU/national/homeland]: Security and defence *and* international crisis management. Once reforms are complete, the armed forces in Spain, Italy, Poland and Germany will produce significantly increased capabilities for the EU, and will reduce the reliance on France and the UK.

EU coordination in armaments development and procurement should, at least in theory, be one of the best ways to build new capabilities. Under the ESDP, the EU's national armaments directors meet regularly and the institutionalisation of this format, a European Armaments Agency, makes sense. Cooperation is further developed within the ECAP framework. However, this element of the ESDP has at the same time been one of its least rewarding aspects. National prestige, industry concerns and the need to preserve jobs mean that this is a highly political issue. Coordination within the EU challenges other established defence-cooperation forums (WEAG, OCCAR and the separate defence-industrial cooperation under the 'letter-of-intent' process among the EU's six largest defence producers).

Intensified defence-industrial cooperation is nonetheless essential to the ESDP, and crucial if Europe is to increase its military capabilities. There is massive duplication and over-capacity in Europe's defence industries, and quality is frequently lower than in the US. Only through further consolidation, greater competition and more standardised products can Europe hope to increase not only quantitative capability levels, but also qualitative levels. This is also a prerequisite for healthy transatlantic defence procurement.[9] Only when Europe is competitive is the US likely to take it seriously in both the security and defence-industrial arenas.

François Heisbourg has observed that deficiencies in European capabilities are not due to inadequate overall defence spending.[10] EU member states spent 173.5bn euros ($156bn) on defence in 2001.[11] Heisbourg argues that Europeans can improve the *efficiency* of their defence spending by defining force goals, improving budget structures and input criteria (for example, convergence criteria) and the pooling of key capabilities.[12] Given that force planning boils down to national interests, policies and priorities, there is little reason to believe that EU defence planning will significantly better NATO's in realising capabilities. Nevertheless, a 'Europeanisation' of defence planning and force goals is bound to occur, and could lead to a more coordinated approach to European capabilities development.

Europe has huge arsenals of assets; EU member states have almost 9,000 main battle tanks, for instance (this number more than doubles if Turkey and EU-candidate countries are included), more than 50 conventional submarines and more than 3,000 combat aircraft, but only a fraction of these assets could be categorised as capabilities for real crisis-management operations. There is thus massive duplication. The problem is that European states, most of which declare that they have moved on from the concept of conventional territorial defence, continue to invest in traditional equipment without looking at what they really need for crisis-management operations. As pooling and functional coordination is practically non-existent, any improvement through defence planning, dialogue and cooperation would be a step in the right direction.

Joint requirements and joint procurement can result in additional and cheaper assets, hopefully of a high technological standard. Above all, pooling key national capabilities could significantly increase European capabilities. It does not make sense that almost every European state has its own C-130 and/or C-160 airlift assets and full logistic support and training, however small the force. The German idea of a joint EU transport command is sound and should be developed, as should the NATO Prague Capabilities Commitment of November 2002 which called for the pooling and joint ownership of support jamming pods, air-to-air refuelling and UAVs. Leasing or buying US strategic airlift also makes sense. Pooling would also be relevant for sealift, some aircraft logistics (for the F-16, *Mirage*, *Tornado*, *Eurofighter* and an array of helicopters), military medical services, air and maritime control and submarine search and rescue.[13] Functions such as naval and air patrols could also be coordinated, at least in sub-regions. As the protection of external borders is increasingly seen as a common mission, a standing European naval force and coast guard tasked with defence and border control may emerge.

Pooling higher military education and specialist training, and the consequent closing down of some national facilities, can save money and increase quality and interoperability. Similarly, it could be possible to merge national defence-research establishments. Although the gradual consolidation of Europe's defence industries will generate more multinational research and development, governments must seek European cooperation in research beyond multinational procurement programmes.[14]

Role specialisation may *de facto* occur in all European armed forces, but few states are prepared to develop a formal policy. Coordination and the sharing of tasks with trusted neighbours, with Benelux cooperation as a model, is a more palatable option until further European integration permits bolder steps. Sub-regional cooperation – as in EUROCORPS, EUROMARFOR, ARRC and the Nordic Brigade – adds multinational capabilities that are interoperable and relevant, while enhancing commonality and spreading political risk and cost. The NRF may prove a useful instrument not only for the rational coordination of high-readiness capabilities, but also for NATO cohesion, transatlantic interoperability and European insight into US force transformation.

Increased attention is also being paid to doctrinal, operational and technical interoperability. The development of doctrines for military crisis management is done better and more economically in a multinational framework. In general, exercises and training should increasingly be multinational – even at relatively low tactical levels. National 'jointness', an area in which a majority of

EU member states still face enormous challenges, should develop towards multinational European 'jointness'. NATO standardisation is, for now, the key instrument of this process, although EU operations will demand interoperability and 'jointness' at lower levels than are called for in traditional NATO deployments. The NRF may come to play a role even in this sense. Interoperability efforts within the alliance and Europe must be accelerated; one aspect of this is increased quality control and the tactical evaluation of capabilities committed to EU and NATO service.

Exercises may seem an obvious step towards interoperability. Although there is an EU policy in this area, it engages only EU and NATO strategic-level structures, not operational and tactical capabilities and live exercises. Military units committed to the Headline Goal, including non-NATO headquarters, should exercise together. Cooperation in the Balkans helps, but only when units exercise together can they function together immediately on deployment. This calls for specific forces and units to be assigned to the Headline Goal, not just the commitment of a force whose specific composition and field partner is decided on a case-by-case basis.[15] This is an area where healthy EU–NATO cooperation can be developed in practice.

In the civilian crisis-management field, it is equally important to follow through on capability initiatives. Further steps will demand increased cooperation and coordination. Police officers for crisis-management operations are the spearhead of this cooperation, and common principles, concepts and training are being applied. Nevertheless, there is work to be done. The EU's police catalogue must differentiate between different kinds of police for different deployments. Common concepts are also being developed for rule-of-law elements. Cooperation is embryonic in EU civilian crisis management, but the potential for development is limited only by the imagination, and issues of national prestige and cost. Cooperation in the wake of national disasters in Europe has highlighted the need for coordination among neighbours, and demonstrated that some of the capabilities needed for out-of-area crisis management are equally relevant at home.

Conceptually and in practice, progress has been impressive in just a few short years. In the area of border control, the idea of a

European corps of border guards is already being debated.[16] Developing *gendarmerie*-type forces, and increasing European cooperation among them, could add an important counter-terrorism capability and a capability much in demand in peace-support operations. Capabilities cannot easily be tailored either for domestic purposes or for out-of-area operations since operational needs tend to override such definitions. Increased coordination and cooperation between border guards, coast guards, area surveillance, *gendarmerie* forces and the police makes sense, and prepares Europe for challenges both within and outside the Union.

Capability initiatives, both regional and pan-European alike, are also affected by EU enlargement. To give an example, the Baltic Sea region will be fundamentally transformed with the enlargement of the EU so that all states except Russia are members. Cooperation and coordination in what will become an 'EU lake' will in time probably affect police cooperation, border control, military environmental issues, sea and air surveillance (civilian and military), intelligence coordination, the joint monitoring of threats from organised crime and terrorists, search and rescue and practical interoperability for all elements involved. There are also significant financial and political gains to be derived from such regional coordination, not to mention advantages in European integration. As internal and external security become difficult to separate, so the need for national and regional coordination between such elements as police services, coast guards, navies and customs will increase. Just as security cooperation between Belgium, the Netherlands and Luxembourg has developed since the Second World War, so this is gradually spreading across Europe. In all probability, we have seen only the beginning. New security-related areas of cooperation are bound to emerge.

Developing joint non-military and military crisis management capabilities

The EU also faces the challenge of linking non-military and military crisis management and developing joint capabilities in order to broaden the range of tools for managing crises. There is a need to link military and non-military crisis-management capabilities at both the strategic and the operational level. Whether or not the

Political and Security Committee evolves into a EU Security Council, it must coordinate all elements of crisis management, including
non-military components. The two elements should be inseparable
in conceptual work, planning and operational command-and-control.[17] Currently, the EU lacks any kind of command-and-control
arrangement for non-military operations. Unity of command, from
the political level down to the field operators, must be established
across the whole crisis-management spectrum.

EU states should identify and catalogue the relevant civilian
capabilities as has been done for military capabilities. Within the
various categories, a minimum of standardisation and interoperability should be established between national capabilities, and
between multinational capabilities. Joint training and exercises are
also necessary, as is the development of day-to-day coordination
mechanisms among states and between states and the EU non-
military crisis-management structure.

Taking the Headline Goal idea one step further, EU civil
protection and crisis management would benefit from the establishment of 'Reaction Packages'. For example, readily-available
Packages should be tailored to emergency relief in the wake of
natural or man-made disasters, both within the EU and externally.
This may involve linking national and international NGOs and
relief agencies with civilian and military medical support, military
engineering, search-and-rescue capabilities and military transport.
Some Packages could be based on modular rapid-reaction police
forces, while others could focus on civil emergencies, medical or
search-and-rescue (non-military and military) operations. Pre-crisis
state-building elements should also be available in 'Package' form.
Another niche could be threat-reduction teams for detection and
monitoring, or joint teams dealing with radiological, biological or
chemical terrorist attacks. Post-crisis detoxification and sanitisation
is another field. Fact-finding teams and several of the Reaction
Packages must be capable of reacting immediately.

At the higher end of the crisis spectrum, there should be
Reaction Packages for initial deployments of humanitarian missions, evacuation operations, peace-support operations and post-
conflict state-building. The scenarios for such contingencies exist,
but not the pre-identification of capabilities earmarked for them.

Some Reaction Packages would contain mainly conventional military capabilities, while others would focus on unconventional warfare, including special forces (both military and police) for counter-terrorism operations or countering asymmetrical threats. Naturally some capabilities or functions can be earmarked for more than one Package, at least to a certain extent and as long as a level of interoperability is guaranteed.

Size and readiness would naturally vary. Large combat-capable Reaction Packages, perhaps of divisional size, could resemble NATO's joint response force or the Standing Naval Forces, although they would contain a broader range of capabilities (including non-military elements) and standards for interoperability (because of multinationality at lower levels), and pre-readiness training would need to be higher. Another such Reaction Package could be small and highly specialised, more comparable to existing US and UK special-forces cooperation or amphibious-forces cooperation between the UK and the Netherlands. Unity of command, interoperability and the sustainability of non-military and military capabilities are vital, as these would represent the EU's initial engagement forces. If modes of cooperation are established through exercises and dialogue in peacetime, the operational phase is likely to be more effective.

Establishing Reaction Packages cannot happen overnight, and there are significant costs involved as soon as the aim is high readiness. However, most of the assets and capabilities already exist, and many of the components are committed to the Helsinki Headline Goal or could be assembled with existing national capabilities. However, there needs to be more coordination. Since many threats are commonly shared, this could be best achieved in a pan-European or EU forum. Starting off with a couple of Reaction Packages would be a realistic step, and could be a suitable follow-on Headline Goal.

It may be relatively easy to generate the political will for such coordination at the central EU level. The real challenge lies with individual member states. Each government needs to ask itself whether it is prepared to go beyond the current EU commitments, commit to training and maintain in a state of readiness, deal with legal and procedural obstacles to taking quick decisions. Is there a real interest in sending non-military assets abroad and developing the capability to contribute to quick and effective decision-making in Brussels on conflict prevention and crisis management? Some governments may fear the misguided label of 'EU Army' that could be applied to these pre-identified, pre-trained and interoperable Reaction Packages. On the other hand, many of the challenges described above are as important within the Union as they are globally, and in most cases multinational cooperation is essential for effective engagement. The institutional label is less important than the development of coordinated European capabilities. For now, the EU looks to be the most suitable forum for such coordination, though the EU should also seek broader international cooperation. Coordination with any NATO response force or operational capability is inevitable and should be encouraged. In civil emergencies, there is every reason to build on NATO's experience in Kosovo and Macedonia. In counter-terrorism, cooperation with the US should be a priority.

A practical approach to EU–NATO cooperation

A close and effective institutional working relationship between the EU and NATO would be sensible and logical. However, this will not materialise unless it is in the interests of all member states.[18] EU–NATO cooperation requires not only formal agreement on the political front, but also strategic compatibility and practical arrangements, for which the identification of common strategic objectives,[19] compatible procedures and over-arching priorities is key. This should be done at the highest political level.[20]

In an ideal world, the joint EU–NATO forum should be broadened to include all levels of cooperation, from groups of experts and ambassadors to foreign and defence ministers and heads of state and government. In areas of common interest, and where there is broad Western consensus, the joint forum should also have decision-making powers.[21] The bottom line is that the EU and NATO member states should be flexible, and use whatever institution, forum or group is relevant for the issue at hand. The major drawbacks with such a forum are that it would limit 'constructive ambiguity' between the two institutions, for states belonging to both organisations to present only one point of view (rather than different positions for each group), and add yet another layer of decision-making. However, even if the only result is dialogue, confidence-building, institutional coordination and decision-shaping between the two institutions, European security would still benefit.[22]

The alternative to a close EU–NATO relationship lies in accentuated bilateral ties – first and foremost the EU–US relationship. This could be supported, for example, by augmenting the suggested EU Security Council with an American representative on a case-by-case or functional basis. Points of contact between the EU and EU-candidate countries are also important. In time – and depending on EU cohesion post enlargement, the follow-on to the ESDP, a new form of burden-sharing across the Atlantic and cooperation on issues of common concern – the EU–US relationship may become the core not only of European, but also Western, security cooperation. The EU, because of the wide spectrum of security-projecting elements at its disposal, may become a more important dialogue partner for the US than the more narrowly focused European pillar in NATO. Nevertheless, the functions and capabilities should be in focus, not institutional labels. Over the next decade or so, the wisest course is to develop both close EU–NATO and close EU–US relations, with the aim of sustaining NATO as an organisation and exploiting the many useful elements of cooperation, including the benefits of engaging non-EU NATO members in European and EU crisis management.

EU–NATO cooperation in defence and operational planning

The EU will need to develop its own defence-planning process. Called the Capabilities Development Mechanism, this will largely mirror NATO's defence-planning process. Just as in NATO, there is a need within the EU to link collective goals and scenarios to force catalogues, procurement and operationalising capabilities, and progress reviews. Three challenges should be addressed.

First, while it will be difficult to merge the two defence-planning processes or integrate EU defence planning into NATO's, it would nonetheless make sense if both the EU and NATO member states could at least identify compatible political goals (NATO

Ministerial Guidance and EU Headline Goals), directions and priorities. Differences relating to strategic and operational needs (for example, different requirements for strategic intelligence and deployment range and different roles in territorial defence) and different linkages to defence-industrial policies and national agendas ought to be manageable as long as the aim is compatibility, not trying to make the two processes identical or one and the same. At the very least, the two defence-planning cycles should be synchronised and the processes should be parallel. When it comes to EU and NATO defence planning, there should be nothing to hide between the two organisations and, although non-member decision-shaping in defence planning may be limited, transparency and compatibility should be complete.

Just as has been the case for NATO, the EU process must permit opt-outs, without individual states being able to obstruct cooperation among the majority. In the case of obstruction by a minority, an alternative for those states that want to cooperate is to create a defence-planning process which is formally separate from the EU and NATO, but which uses the same mechanism and processes.

Second, in practical crisis management contacts between the EU and NATO should be developed at all levels and in all possible forums – particularly between military staff and the decision-making bodies. The alternative, should individual states obstruct such dialogue, is to create *ad hoc* arrangements outside the EU or NATO, or to use bilateral and multilateral contacts. Although this would damage institutional cohesion, it would also permit pragmatic and sensible cooperation.

Third, it is the responsibility of the individual member states, not the institutions, to produce the capabilities required. Although institutional staff can coordinate national defence planning and provide collective processes, every state will remain loyal to its own national interests and domestic agendas. As each state has only one defence-planning process, one set of forces and one procurement budget, it is up to individual nations to ensure that the substance of the two defence-planning processes remains the same, even though the two processes may cater to different roles and goals.

At the operational level, once the political decision has been made to initiate planning and to invite non-members to participate, all states engaged in an operation should be involved. This could mean troop contributors from non-NATO EU members participating in NATO planning, or non-EU NATO member states in EU planning. To safeguard NATO's valuable capability in operational planning, SHAPE and the Combined Joint Planning Staff should be opened up to non-NATO EU members, which should enjoy a status similar to that of the French, with national representatives in Mons. Differing transatlantic operational agendas and intelligence assessments may prove a challenge, but increased European intelligence capabilities and US–EU intelligence cooperation should minimise the problem.

Ideally, NATO and EU operational planning should be amalgamated and a formula found to ensure that no one member state can stop the others from cooperating. European operational planning could be produced by NATO staff – as long as the staff can also produce autonomous EU operational alternatives and credibly serve the EU without a US/NATO political slant. Effective contacts should be established between the EU Military Staff, the Combined Joint Planning Staff and the prime European operational headquarters. The principle of reciprocity is important. Just as the EU can rely on NATO assets and capabilities, so NATO must be able to count on EU assets and capabilities. Special arrangements would have to be made for NATO's Article 5 and nuclear planning.

This paper does not advocate the development of a European joint-operations headquarters akin to SHAPE in its calibre and role. As long as there is guaranteed access by the EU and all its member states to SHAPE, the Combined Joint Planning Staff and related capabilities, there is little reason for duplication. However, if that is not the case, a 'Euro-SHAPE' may well be developed in the longer term. The advantage would be not having to rely on the veto of non-EU NATO members; and within the union, not to have to rely on a UK-, French- or German-dominated national operational headquarters. A European HQ should be able to handle both civilian and military crisis-management capabilities, a point that will become increasingly important the more military and civilian crisis-management capabilities are coordinated at the strategic and operational level. If such a European HQ was purely military, it would compete with SHAPE and only complicate common operational perceptions and planning transparency. The main challenge with a European HQ would lie in operational cooperation with the US. US cooperation through both SHAPE and a European HQ sounds complicated, but may be manageable.

EU–NATO cooperation is not technically or practically difficult – the obstacles are purely political. Theoretically, if there is the political will, then effective EU–NATO cooperation could be established, even in the short term.

Conclusion

Policy coordination in the CFSP and ESDP has developed since 1999 and today the EU is a net exporter of security. The Union is well placed to link a wide palette of economic, diplomatic and military means in the fight against multifaceted threats and challenges. It is a unique forum for coordination and consultation across nations, borders, sectors and institutions. The EU has the potential to become a global force in conflict prevention and crisis management. While the EU may not manage potential or active crises in the same way, or using the same instruments, as the US or a US-led coalition, it may potentially become a valued strategic partner where common values and interests are at stake. However, without the development of more relevant capabilities, and increased European coordination Europe will be limited to yesterday's tools for tomorrow's challenges.

Currently, the military capabilities of EU member states fall short of their declared ambitions, and will do so for years to come. Relying on current institutions, processes, defence-budget levels and defence planning, Europe will, at best, see only marginal increases in its military capabilities over the next five years. The picture is brighter regarding non-military/civilian crisis-management capabilities. However, significant political obstacles complicate efforts to enhance the EU's overall capabilities, both in the civilian and military fields.

The US and NATO have offered their support and cooperation. It is now up to the UK, France, Germany and the other EU member states to improve and better coordinate their efforts to produce enhanced capabilities and, ultimately, achieve an increase in the substantive level of European contributions to regional and worldwide security fully commensurate with the role, interests and resources of the EU and its members. It would help if the debate on increasing European crisis-management capabilities focused less on institutional labelling, fanciful notions of European global power projection, a 'European Army' or supposed challenges to the US and NATO, and instead identified how European states can realistically increase their capacity for effective conflict prevention and crisis management. Most of all, Europe needs better mechanisms and processes for coordinating national capabilities.

Despite slow progress in implementing the NATO Defence Capabilities Initiative and the EU Helsinki Headline Goal, the Europeans will in 2003 possess a large, albeit traditionally-structured, force reservoir. The EU member states will essentially be capable of performing all the military tasks that fall explicitly within the Petersberg spectrum, including peace enforcement. For complex operations demanding a high operational tempo, reduced risks to EU forces and minimum collateral damage, Europe will, for the rest of the decade, still depend on US assets. Strategic sea and airlift, intelligence assets and all-weather precision-strike capabilities are further prerequisites for major high-tempo operations.

Over the next few years, quantitative and qualitative improvements in reconnaissance, communications, strategic lift, air-to-air refuelling, tactical mobility, force protection, combat search and rescue, electronic counter-measures, theatre-missile defence, UAVs, precision-guided munitions, NBC protection and logistics will indicate how far the NATO and EU capabilities initiatives have succeeded, and to what extent the prospects of EU operational autonomy for larger combat operations are going to be realised. In any case, several years will normally elapse between the appropriation of funds and the availability of new operational capabilities. So far, the impact of the DCI and the Headline Goal on European force modernisation has been limited. It remains to be seen if the November 2002 NATO Prague Capabilities Commitment will generate more than a marginal additional increase.

Real increases in European military capabilities will derive not only from the acquisition of new assets, but also from innovative organisational approaches. There is great potential in the pooling of assets and capabilities, rationalisation and multinational cooperation in military education and training, doctrinal development, logistical support and defence-industrial consolidation. Joint procurement and production and far-reaching pooling initiatives – from air transport, electronic warfare, maintenance and logistics to defence-research establishments – will save money and produce more interoperable and flexible capabilities. It takes several years for multinational formations to become truly effective and operational. Action must be taken soon, or the opportunity to increase European capabilities in this decade will be lost. The price for such action will be paid mainly in national prestige, as the desire for national ownership of defence assets and industries dies hard. Unilateral engagement against the will of partners and allies will also become more difficult once multinational development, procurement and pooling are the norm.

'Jointness' and interoperability within NATO remain key challenges. The transatlantic technological and doctrinal gap will not close given the rapid pace at which the US is acquiring new high-tech assets. The European focus on crisis management and peace support is in stark contrast to the US attention to high-tech warfare and homeland defence. Of course, the responsibility for keeping forces interoperable and enabling them to reap the benefits of 'jointness' rests on both sides. This is likely to be an issue of transatlantic debate and finger-pointing. The standards of US-led war-fighting coalitions and NATO peace enforcement will not necessarily be the same as those for EU-led operations. The new NATO Response Force may bridge part of the gap. European interest and European access to US transformational technology and doctrine will determine the level of success.

The EU's dependence on NATO (as opposed to US) assets and capabilities is actually marginal. Although NATO's UK-led rapid-reaction corps is the most effective corps headquarters in Europe, the only collective NATO capability upon which the EU depends is the operational planning capacity in SHAPE's Combined Joint Planning Staff. National planning and command-and-control capabilities exist in the UK, France and Germany. This means that the EU is in fact not vitally dependent on NATO's collective assets. Even 'SHAPE-like' multinational planning capabilities could if necessary be duplicated within the EU.

Nevertheless, NATO's established military-integration structures provide an indispensable framework for the transition to enhanced European forces capable of full-spectrum operations. NATO is likely to remain relevant to the EU even after its dependence on US forces becomes less pronounced than today. In the interest of reaching the EU's declared capability goals, practical contacts between the EU and NATO must be developed at all levels, particularly between military staff and decision-makers. There is value in working towards synchronised defence planning in parallel in NATO and the EU. The EU would greatly benefit from live exercises to develop its operational and tactical capabilities.

European capability-building efforts must be evaluated on their own merits, and in their own timeframe. The EU's comparative advantage lies not in high-intensity warfare, but in conflict prevention through the coordinated use of diplomatic and economic measures, and crisis management with civilian and military means. It would be a mistake to judge the EU's military capabilities in isolation from its other crisis-prevention and conflict-management capabilities. For many scenarios, improvements in decision-making and the determined application of the economic, diplomatic and civilian elements of crisis management could prove just as important, if not more so, than war-fighting capabilities. Increasingly, the capabilities needed for such operations are just as relevant for many internal challenges, such as civil emergency support, man-made and natural disasters and the fight against terrorism.

The development of crisis management in the spheres of civil protection and conflict prevention is particularly important. Significant progress has already been made in the EU, but there is vast potential for additional measures to strengthen the EU's ability to deal with disasters, build coordinated European police and *gendarmerie* capabilities, promote the rule of law in areas of instability, conduct observer missions and defence diplomacy and share intelligence on threats and risks from terrorism, critical-infrastructure attacks and weapons of mass destruction. In combining such capabilities with its diplomatic, economic, financial and military potential, Europe has much to offer. Close coordination between the civilian and military elements of crisis management, including establishing pre-trained, interoperable and high-readiness Reaction Packages, would further enhance Europe's ability to employ its widely-defined power to the benefit of international peace and security.

The core challenge is to develop the EU's political cohesion and strategic decision-making capability, linking the various elements together in common long-term policies. Only when trade, diplomatic initiatives, loan policies, national NGO initiatives and regional relations are combined can conflict prevention succeed. It would also make sense to coordinate issues such as defence-industrial cooperation, technology transfer and intelligence at the strategic EU level. Today's EU lacks a command and control establishment even for civilian operations. To turn the EU as a whole into a strategic actor, unity of command would first have to be assured across the crisis-management spectrum, from the political level down to field operations. In the complex relationship between member states and community institutions across the EU's three pillars, the question of who is in command must be resolved.

Eventually, one body needs to be coordinating all civilian and military elements of the ESDP and the EU's external relations. Such an 'EU Security Council' would go a long way to overcoming the well-known shortcomings that have prevented the EU from being seen as a strategic actor: insufficient coordination between the three pillars, inadequate civil–military integration, ill-defined interests and policies, insufficient efforts to build public support and a failure to actively seek wide coordination and dialogue with other governments and international organisations – above all the US – in early, proactive engagement, initiative, risk-taking and leadership.

Autonomous strategic decision-making and military self-sustainability in intelligence – both declared goals of the EU – also call for proper EU intelligence capabilities, including CFSP ESDP-specific assessments and analysis. Effective conflict prevention in the pre-crisis phase demands high-quality and multifaceted intelligence. Further operational intelligence is necessary for any crisis-management engagement. There is a growing need for a centrally-coordinated EU intelligence function modelled on the UK's Joint Intelligence Committee, and a fundamental reassessment of intelligence cooperation requirements in Europe.

Capabilities development is not about autonomy, national posturing or grand visions of power projection. Mere quantities of assets and institutional labels are of little use. What it is really about is rational coordination within Europe, pragmatic cooperation between the EU and NATO and between the EU and the US, and the development of a combined ability to project security internally and externally. The outcome will depend, more than anything else, on the quality of political relations between the EU and the US. European capabilities, both civilian and military, are likely to advance faster and with more success if transatlantic relations focus on generating improved abilities to act jointly in preventing crises, countering threats, managing conflicts, supporting stability and enhancing international peace and security.

Appendix

Table 1 Selected military ESDP capabilities (as committed in 2002)

	Land forces	Aircraft	Ships	Other
EU member states				
Austria	1 mechanised infantry battalion 1 light-infantry battalion 1 NBC defence/SAR unit 1 transport company 1 CIMIC unit 1 humanitarian assistance package 100 observers	1 medical/transport helicopter squadron		
Belgium	1 mechanised infantry brigade	1 squadron (12) F-16s 8 C-130s 2 Airbus	2 frigates 6 mine-countermeasure vessels (MCMV) 1 command/support ship	
Denmark	None	None	None	None
Finland	HQ component 1 mechanised infantry battalion 1 engineer battalion 1 transport company 1 civil-military cooperation (CIMIC) group Logistics/support Military observers		1 mine-countermeasures command/support ship	
France	1 light-infantry brigade 1 armoured brigade	75 combat aircraft 24 carrier-based combat aircraft	1 nuclear-powered attack submarine	Various headquarters C4ISR

(Continued to p. 114)

	Land forces	Aircraft	Ships	Other
France continued	1 airborne brigade 1 amphibious brigade Special forces NBC defence support Multiple-launch rocket system (MLRS) Electronic-warfare support Reconnaissance systems	2 carrier-based reconnaissance aircraft 2 AWACS aircraft 8 tanker aircraft 3 long-range transport aircraft 24 mid-range transport aircraft SAR helicopters 3 maritime patrol aircraft	1 aircraft carrier 2 large amphibious ships 4 frigates (1 air defence) 3 support ships Ship-borne medical support	Satellite imagery
Germany	7 combat battalions 8 air-defence squadrons 1 CIMIC unit 2 signals-intelligence units 1 information-operations unit Reconnaissance/surveillance systems Support elements 2 field hospitals	7 squadrons combat aircraft (1 naval) Air transport Sea surveillance	13 combat vessels 1 ship-borne hospital	Various headquarters
Greece	1 HQ 1 mechanised infantry brigade 1 light-infantry battalion 1 Patriot air-defence battalion 1 MLRS battalion 1 short-range air-defence (SHORAD) squadron	1 combat helicopter company 1 transport helicopter company 42 combat aircraft 4 transport aircraft 1 maritime patrol aircraft	8 combat vessels 2 amphibious ships 2 auxiliary ships	
Ireland	1 light infantry battalion Special-forces group			

	Land forces	Aircraft	Ships	Other
Italy	2 mechanised brigades (with mountain option) 1 airmobile brigade 1 amphibious infantry battalion 1 engineering battalion 1 NBC defence company 1 CIMIC group Special forces 2 SHORAD units Military police units	6 carrier-based AV8B combat aircraft 8 carrier-based helicopters 8 amphibious support helicopters 26 Tornado and AMX combat aircraft 6 combat SAR helicopters 9 transport aircraft 2 tanker aircraft 3 maritime patrol aircraft	1 aircraft carrier 1 destroyer 3 frigates 4 patrol vessels/corvettes 1 submarine 4 MCMVs 1 mine-countermeasures command/support ship 2 amphibious ships 1 support ship 1 oceanographic vessel 2 coast guard vessels	Various headquarters C3I
Luxembourg	1 light reconnaissance unit			
Netherlands	Headquarters component 1 mechanised infantry/airmobile brigade 1 amphibious battalion Air defence	3 squadrons F-16s Transport aircraft	1 landing platform dock Frigates (air-defence, command, multipurpose)	
Portugal	1 infantry brigade 1 marine battalion Military observers	1 squadron (12) F-16s 4 C-130s 16 C-130/C-212s 3 maritime patrol aircraft 4 SA/330 helicopters	1 frigate 1 submarine 1 patrol boat 1 support ship 1 survey ship	Tactical air control
Sweden	1 mechanised infantry battalion 1 engineer company	1 squadron (4) reconnaissance aircraft	2 corvettes 2 command/support vessels	

	Land forces	Aircraft	Ships	Other
Sweden continued	1 military police company Military observers	4 C-130s 1 electronic warfare/signals-intelligence aircraft	1 submarine 2 MCMVs	
Spain	1 mechanised brigade 1 marine brigade 1 mountain battalion 1 light-infantry battalion 1 special-forces battalion	2 squadrons (24) F-1/F-18 combat aircraft 1 naval air unit 1 squadron (9) CN-235s reconnaissance aircraft tanker aircraft medical-evacuation aircraft electronic-warfare aircraft	1 aircraft carrier 4 amphibious vessels 2 frigates 1 support vessel	Various headquarters
UK	1 armoured/mechanised/airborne brigade 1 amphibious brigade Artillery SHORAD Logistics/support 1 field hospital	72 combat aircraft 58 strategic transport aircraft Chinook/Merlin transport helicopters attack helicopters	1 aircraft carrier 2 nuclear-powered submarines 4 destroyers/frigates 1 helicopter carrier 6 ro-ro support vessels 2 landing platform docks	1 mobile joint headquarters Mobile communications

	Land forces	Aircraft	Ships	Other
Non-EU European NATO member states				
Czech Republic	1 mechanised infantry battalion 1 special-forces company 1 field hospital 1 humanitarian/rescue operations centre	1 transport helicopter unit		
Hungary	1 mechanised infantry battalion 1 SHORAD platoon			
Iceland	Up to 50 civilian personnel			
Norway	3,500 troops			
Poland	Framework brigade (HQ elements) 1 infantry battalion Engineering company Military police section)	SAR elements 1 An-28 transport aircraft	2 MCMVs	
Turkey	1 mechanised brigade	2 F-16 squadrons 2 C-130/C-160s	2 frigates 1 submarine 1 support vessel 1 amphibious ship 1 MCMV	

	Land forces	Aircraft	Ships	Other
Others				
Bulgaria	1 mechanised battalion 1 NBC defence company 1 reconnaissance company 1 military field hospital 1 humanitarian refugee centre	1 helicopter squadron		
Cyprus	1 transport company	1 medium-altitude reconnaissance and surveillance system		Infrastructure in Cyprus
Estonia	Component of the Baltic battalion 1 infantry battalion 1 military police group 1 explosive ordnance disposal unit CIMIC personnel		2 MCMVs 1 support ship	
Latvia	Component of the Baltic battalion 1 infantry battalion 1 explosive-ordnance disposal unit 1 medical team 1 military police unit		1 MCMV	
Lithuania	Component of the Baltic battalion Component of the Lithuanian-Polish battalion 1 mechanised infantry battalion	1 helicopter 2 aircraft	2 MCMVs 2 vessels	

	Land forces	Aircraft	Ships	Other
Romania	1 mechanised battalion 1 engineering battalion 1 military-police company 1 mountain-infantry company Special forces (1 diving team)		4 vessels	
Slovakia	1 mechanised company 1 engineering unit 1 military-police unit 1 field hospital	4 Mi-17 transport helicopters		
Slovenia	1 mechanised company 1 military-police unit 1 medical unit	1 transport helicopter		

Sources: IISS, *The Military Balance 2002–2003* (Oxford: Oxford University Press for the IISS, 2002); national press releases; *Atlantic News,* 21 November 2001; *Jane's Defence Weekly,* 12 December 2001.

Notes

Acknowledgements

The author would like to thank Klaus Becher, Helmut Schmidt Senior Fellow for European Security at the IISS. For valuable input and comments on drafts, thanks also to Alyson Bailes, Giles Baldwin, Hans Binnendijk, Lawrence Freedman, Nils Gyldén, François Heisbourg, Björn Müller-Wille, Alessandro Politi, Sven Rudberg, Lars Wedin and Erik Windmar. Mats Berdal, Katarina Engberg and Bo Huldt have also been greatly supportive.

Introduction

[1] For historical background on the European Security and Defence Policy (ESDP) and initial debate around it, see: François Heisbourg, *European Defence: Making It Work*, Chaillot Paper 42 (Paris: WEU Institute for Security Studies, 2000); Jolyon Howorth, *European Integration and Defence: The Ultimate Challenge?*, Chaillot Paper 43 (Paris: WEU Institute for Security Studies, 2000); Alyson Bailes, 'NATO's European Pillar: The European Security and Defense Identity', *Defense Analysis*, vol. 15, no. 3, 1999; Strobe Talbott 'Transatlantic Ties', *Newsweek*, 18 October 1999; Charles Grant, *European Defence Post Kosovo?* (London: Centre for European Reform, 1999); James Thomas, *The Military Challenges of Transatlantic Coalitions*, Adelphi Paper 333 (Oxford: Oxford University Press for the IISS, 2000).

[2] Where NATO provides assets and capabilities to the EU, political sensitivities have added further facets to these two terms. Here, 'capabilities' describes a function or service, such as information, airborne early warning or access to communications. For EU-led operations, NATO would not transfer capabilities to the EU; NATO would remain in command of its own capabilities even while they are used to support an EU operation. An asset (HQ, units, personnel, specific equipment) could, however, be temporarily transferred to the EU and placed under its control and command for the task at hand. This paper will however use the more generally accepted definitions of capabilities and assets as described in the text.

3 'Military crisis management' encompasses traditional peace-support operations, from preventive deployment and peacekeeping to armed intervention and peace enforcement. It also includes humanitarian and evacuation operations, civil-protection tasks that use mainly military instruments and proactive engagement against weapons of mass destruction and counter-terrorism. Examples include UNPROFOR, embargo operations in the Adriatic, the Sierra Leone operation and military counter-terrorism strikes. Civilian crisis management, as defined by the EU Summit at Feira in June 2000, comprises four areas: police, the rule of law, civil administration and civil protection. The first three are sometimes referred to as 'state-building' activities. Civil protection is essentially humanitarian support in times of crisis, and can include military components such as airlift, medical support and logistics. 'Conflict prevention' is a formal term used officially by the EU. It is defined as the use of primarily non-military means to stabilise a state or a region in the pre-crisis phase (i.e. before the use of force). Initiatives include preventive diplomacy, defence diplomacy, observer missions, the sharing of intelligence and promoting human rights and democracy. Confidence- and security-building measures, arms control and non-proliferation initiatives may also be included.

4 Should vital interests be at stake, states tend to either redefine those interests or go to war, whatever the legal, institutional or multinational context. This paper defines 'vital' interests as interests that are of overriding importance to the survival, safety and vitality of a state.

Chapter 1

1 US aircrews flew just over half of the Kosovo campaign's 10,484 strike missions, delivered 80% of munitions and conducted 70% of support missions. Of the 38,004 sorties flown, Italy accounted for 3%, the UK 4% and France roughly 10%. France and the UK dropped just 4% each of the 23,614 air munitions released by NATO aircraft. Of the 4,397 Suppression of Enemy Air Defence (SEAD) sorties flown, the UK carried out less than half a dozen, and France none. Only the US had long-endurance unmanned aerial vehicles (UAVs), advanced radar-jamming aircraft, strategic bombers, stealth capabilities and battlefield ground surveillance, in the form of the Joint-Surveillance Target Attack Radar System (Joint-STARS). There were, however, gaps in US capabilities as well, particularly in 'jointness', readiness, interoperability, logistics and infrastructure support; several of the above mentioned assets were severely stretched. See Linda Krzaryn, 'Cohen Calls On Allies To Share the Load', *American Forces Press Service*, 8 July 1999; *Report on Allied Contributions to the Common Defense*, A Report to the United States Congress by the Secretary of Defense (Washington DC: Department of Defense, March 2000), pp. II–10; *Kosovo – Lessons from the Crisis* (London: Ministry of Defence, June 2000), Annex F; and *Les Enseignements du Kosovo*, Ministère de la Dèfense; Jeffrey Lewis, *Preliminary Lessons From Operation Allied Force*

(through June 1, 1999) (Washington DC: CSIS, 1999); Dick Diamond *et al.*, *Raytheon Kosovo Lessons Learned Study*, Raytheon Systems Company, 9 September 1999; and *Kosovo Air Operations: Need to Maintain Alliance Cohesion Resulted in Doctrinal Departures*, US General Accounting Office Report GAO-01–784 (Washington DC: USGAO, July 2001).

2 Strategic lift was a major bottleneck. Even the UK's request for airlift support from the US was turned down because of a lack of US assets. The Europeans could not rely on strategic airlift or sealift assets owned by states not sympathetic to the NATO operation, such as Russia and Ukraine.

3 The UK's after-action report noted shortfalls in precision all-weather strike capabilities, strategic lift, intelligence, surveillance and reconnaissance, SEAD, electronic warfare and air-to-air refuelling. The French assessment focused on pet projects such as conventional cruise missiles, electronic counter-measures, UAVs, intelligence satellites and satellites for global positioning. *Kosovo/Operation Allied Force After-Action Report*, p. 25; Sharon Hobson, 'NATO Allies Agree Need To Upgrade Capability', *Jane's Defence Weekly*, 29 September 1999; *Kosovo – Lessons from the Crisis*, chapter 5; Joseph Fitchett, 'Allies Emphasize Need To Prepare for Kosovo-Style Air Wars', *International Herald Tribune*, 12 November 1999.

4 Elinor Sloan, 'DCI: Responding to the US-led Revolution in Military Affairs', *NATO Review*, Spring/Summer 2000.

5 The flaws exposed during *Operation Allied Force* and set out in the DCI, as well as US criticism of European capabilities, were balanced by a report to the US Senate from the US General Accounting Office. The report, issued in September 1999, concluded that, during the 1990s, the allies had made their armed forces more mobile and deployable. The majority of European NATO states had increased their air and sealift, in-flight refuelling, interoperability and precision-strike capabilities. The GAO report concluded that the Europeans had done what they had agreed to do in the 1991 NATO Strategic Concept. *NATO: Progress Toward More Mobile and Deployable Forces*, Report to the Chairman and Ranking Minority Member, Subcommittee on Defense, Committee on Appropriations, US Senate (GAO/NSIAD-99–299 NATO), September 1999. Since then, however, institutional ambition and peer pressure have both increased.

6 NATO's Supreme Headquarters Allied Powers Europe (SHAPE) produced over 200 recommendations some months after the Kosovo campaign, and not surprisingly gave added support to the DCI. According to SHAPE, major flaws lay in nations contributing strike aircraft lacking the full spectrum of targeting capabilities, targeting training, battle-damage-assessment capabilities and intelligence data-processing systems. The North Atlantic Council (NAC)'s procedure for approving targets was criticised as too complicated and slow. Member states' national operational planning was not fully integrated with NATO's, and there was no comprehensive campaign plan. SHAPE also noted the need for a NATO information-operations doctrine, and for more

legal advisers at NATO headquarters.

[7] See Susan Ellis, 'NATO Prepared for New Multi-threat Security Environment', USIA, 16 April 1999; Hans-Christian Hagman, *NATOs Strategiska Koncept 1999*, MUST EXO 5/99, J2 (Stockholm: Swedish Armed Forces HQ, 1999), chapter 3.2; and Hans-Christian Hagman, *Europeiska Militära Krishanteringsförmågor*, EXO 11/99, 10433:74782, J2 (Stockholm: Swedish Armed Forces HQ, 13 December 1999), chapter 3.3.

[8] See Hagman, *Europeiska Militära Krishanteringsförmågor*; Sloan, 'DCI: Responding to the US-led Revolution in Military Affairs'.

[9] Colin Clark and Luke Hill, 'NATO Extends Defense Capabilities Initiative to Partners', *Defense News*, 10 January 2000.

[10] See *Report on Allied Contributions to the Common Defense*.

[11] *Kosovo/Operation Allied Force After-Action Report*, pp. 25–26.

[12] See Lawrence Freedman, *The Revolution in Strategic Affairs*, Adelphi Paper 318 (Oxford: Oxford University Press for the IISS, 1998); Yves Boyer, 'Joint Vision 2010 and the Allies: When Conventional Wisdom Meets Strategic Issues', *RUSI Journal*, April 2000; Michael Codner, 'Some European Concerns About Joint Vision 2010', *ibid.*, April 2000.

[13] Luke Hill, 'TMD: NATO Starts the Countdown', *Jane's Defence Weekly*, 3 January 2001.

[14] See *Report on Allied Contributions to the Common Defense*.

[15] According to the Petersberg Declaration of 1992, and later the Treaty on the European Union, these would include 'humanitarian and rescue tasks; peacekeeping tasks; [and] tasks of combat forces in crisis management, including peacemaking'.

[16] See *WEU Council of Ministers Audit of Assets and Capabilities for European Crisis Management Operations*, Luxembourg, 23 November 1999. For a more detailed assessment of this and other capabilities reviews, see Hagman, *Europeiska Militära Krishanteringsförmågor*.

[17] As some states had reported entire orders of battle, the WEU staff had to make a 'realistic', albeit subjective, assessment of what could really be committed for Petersberg operations.

[18] Until Helsinki, the collective term for European defence- and security-related initiatives had been the European Security and Defence Identity (ESDI). In 2000, 'Identity' was replaced by 'Policy', and ESDP became the accepted acronym for these EU initiatives.

[19] Annex IV, Presidency Reports to the Helsinki European Council on 'Strengthening the Common European Policy of Security and Defence' and on 'Non-Military Crisis Management of the European Union', Nice, 11–12 December 1999.

[20] See the European Council Declaration on Strengthening the Common European Policy on Security and Defence, Cologne, 4 June 1999, paragraph 1.

[21] Presidency Report on the European Security and Defence Policy, Presidency Conclusion, European Council, Nice, 7–9 December 2000. The UK-originated formula came from the St. Malo declaration, and was also used at the NATO summit in Washington in April 1999. In Cologne, France argued that this formula gave NATO first choice. The word 'where' in the formula 'where NATO as a whole is not engaged' can mean both a geographical limitation (the

Euro-Atlantic area) and a reference to time; the latter is more generally accepted. This double interpretation may in the future limit NATO in relation to the EU in crisis-management operations.

22 Annex IV, Presidency Reports to the Helsinki European Council on 'Strengthening the Common European Policy of Security and Defence' and on 'Non-Military Crisis Management of the European Union'. See Peter Norman, 'Plans for EU Military Force Agreed', *Financial Times*, 7 December 1999.

23 IISS, *The Military Balance 2000/2001* (Oxford: Oxford University Press for the IISS, 2000).

24 For an official point of view, see *EU Military Structures: Military Capabilities Commitment Declaration*, http://ue.eu.int/pesc/military/en/CCC.htm.

25 Presidency Conclusions, European Council, Helsinki, 10 and 11 December 1999.

26 Presidency Conclusions, European Council, Santa Maria da Feira, 19 and 20 June 2000.

27 See Carlo Jean, *An Integrated Civil Police Force for the European Union: Tasks, Profile and Doctrine* (Brussels: Centre for European Policy Studies, 2002).

28 See Graham Messervy-Whiting, 'The European Union's Nascent Military Staff', *RUSI Journal*, December 2000.

29 Presidency Report to the Gothenburg European Council on European Security and Defence Policy, Brussels, 11 June 2001.

30 See the French EU Presidency Report on European Security and Defence Policy, 4 December 2000.

31 Statement on Capabilities, issued at the Meeting of the North Atlantic Council in Defence Ministers Session, June 6, 2002, NATO Press Release (2002)074.

32 See Prague Summit Declaration, Press Release (2002) 127, NATO, November 21, 2002, and Joseph Fitchett, 'U.S. Urges NATO Allies in Prague to Update Forces', *International Herald Tribune*, 21 November 2002.

33 See initial thoughts from Hans Binnendijk, 'A European Spearhead Force Would Bridge the Gap', *International Herald Tribune*, 21 October 2002; and Hans Binnendijk and Richard Kugler, 'Transforming European Forces', *Survival*, vol. 44, no. 3, Autumn 2002.

34 See Charles Grant, 'What role for NATO', Centre for European Reform, November 2002.

35 'Quote/Unquote', *International Herald Tribune*, 29 April 1998.

36 'Britain's Thatcher Attacks EU Force as Folly', *Reuters*, 22 November 2000.

Chapter 2

1 Operating combat aircraft, air- and sealift, carrier battle groups and surface combatants for a year – even for the less-demanding missions – would engage tens of thousands of airmen and sailors. The more demanding missions call for 300 aircraft and 75 surface combatants, requiring a massive support structure.

2 For a half-year deployment (the norm for most contingents), the military unit cannot be used for other missions for 18 months as it must have stand-by readiness and tailored pre-deployment training, time for the operational engagement itself and post-deployment reconstitution and retraining.

3 The Helsinki Headline Goal Task Force (HTF) used NATO definitions for readiness. The same five categories are used by the EU.

4 Statement by General Wesley Clark, Commander-in-Chief US European Command, before the Senate Armed Services Committee, 29 February 2000.

5 No NATO pilots were killed in action, while some 500 Yugoslav civilians were killed as a result of NATO air strikes. Less than 1% of missions led to unintended fatalities (collateral damage). *Kosovo – Lessons from the Crisis*, chapter 7.

6 Presidency Reports to the Helsinki European Council, Annex IV, paragraph 7.

7 Final Communiqué, Ministerial Meeting of the North Atlantic Council, Berlin, 3 June 1996, paragraphs 5–8.

8 Washington Summit Communiqué, 24 April 1999, paragraph 10. Throughout 2000 and 2001, there were lengthy debates within NATO over what had been agreed to in the Berlin-plus package. Often, the term 'asset' was defined as personnel, HQs, units or equipment, which could be temporarily placed under EU control. 'Capabilities' such as sealift, operational planning, intelligence, communications and airborne early warning are thus functions or complete services provided to the EU. These definitions are politicised, and relevant only in the EU–NATO/Berlin-plus context.

9 *Report on Allied Contributions to the Common Defense*, p. II-3.

10 See Frank Boland, 'Force Planning in the New NATO', *NATO Review*, vol. 46, no. 3, Autumn 1998.

11 SHAPE/ARFPS planning for a possible ground engagement in Bosnia began in mid-1992. Since then, a vast array of Balkans-related plans has emerged. See Hagman, *UN–NATO Operational Cooperation in Peacekeeping 1992–1995*, University of London PhD, 1997, chapter 7.

12 The NATO budget in 1999 was $1.6 billion, composed of the civilian budget ($164m), the military budget ($720m) and the NATO Security Investment Program ($734m).

13 The fact that EU scenarios have a geographical limitation is only relevant for generic planning. It could be noted that NATO's Article 5 was related to direct support for US territorial defence. The fact that NATO gave the US political support for its counter-terrorist engagements in Asia did not mean that those operations were NATO operations, or that they reflected a collective response by NATO.

14 For operational force planners such as those in NATO, who did most of the number crunching in order to produce credible force requirements, the level of manipulation was frustrating.

15 By late November 2000, this scenario contained two sub-levels: Separation of Parties by Force; and a case where the mission was to maintain the separation of parties in a 'Stable State' setting. The latter would require only some 20,000 troops.

16 *Operation Deliberate Force* had the support of a warring faction, and the Rapid Reaction Force was deployed on non-hostile territory.

17 'Strategic decision-making' describes processes related to decision-making at the highest level. In the EU, the strategic level is the EU Council, COREPER (with decision-shaping from the Political and Security Committee and the SG/HR), and the European Commission. In NATO, strategic decision-making is the domain of the NAC. Strategic planning, on the other hand, is done by the highest-level

planning staff at the military strategic level, which in NATO means SACEUR. As of 2002, the only EU strategic planning capability lies with the EU Military Staff.

[18] See *EU Presidency Report on the European Security and Defence Policy*. Realistically, the parameters would have been set in London, Paris and Berlin before there was EU agreement to act collectively.

[19] See Messervy-Whiting, 'The European Union's Nascent Military Staff'.

[20] The envisaged command structure would be: Council/EUMC, Operational HQ, Force HQ, tactical HQs/component commands and forces.

[21] See 'Designing an EU Conflict Prevention Capability', summary of the EU–NGO CFSP Contact Group meeting, European Parliament, 19 September 2000.

[22] Lars Wedin, Chief Concepts Branch, EU Military Staff, interview with the author, 2 March 2001.

Chapter 3

[1] Alyson Bailes notes that converging interests do not necessarily and automatically produce joint action or joint approaches. See 'National Interests vs. European Approaches to Crisis Management: A View from Brussels', paper presented at the Swedish Institute of International Affairs Conference 'Making the CFSP Work', Stockholm, 30 September 1999.

[2] Opening Statement before the US Senate Committee on Foreign Relations, 17 January 2001.

[3] See Julian Lindley-French, 'Terms of Engagement', Chaillot Paper 52 (Paris: EU Institute for Security Studies, 2002) and William Drozdiak, 'US Seems Increasingly Uncomfortable With EU Defense Plan', *International Herald Tribune*, 6 March 2000.

[4] Two-way trade was valued at $507bn in 1999. EU investment in the US totalled more than $480bn, and US investment in the EU more than $430bn. See *Strengthening Transatlantic Security – A US Strategy for the 21st Century* (Washington DC: DoD, December 2000); and Ed Gunning, *The Common European Security and Defense Policy (ESDP)* (Washington DC: Atlantic Council of the United States, 10 May 2000).

[5] See Stanley Sloan, *The United States and European Defence*, Chaillot Paper 39 (Paris: WEU Institute for Security Studies, 2000); and then Secretary of State Madeleine Albright's warnings of 'decoupling', 'duplication' and 'discrimination', in Drozdiak, 'US Seems Increasingly Uncomfortable'. See also François Heisbourg, 'European Defence Takes a Leap Forward', *NATO Review*, Spring/Summer 2000; Stafano Silvestri and Andrzej Karkoszka, 'The EU–NATO Connection'; and Nicole Gnesotto and Karl Kaiser, 'European–American Interaction', in Heisbourg, *European Defence: Making It Work*.

[6] See Willem Van Eekelen, *EU, WEU, and NATO: Towards a European Security and Defence Identity*, Defence and Security Committee, North Atlantic Assembly, 22 April 1999, paragraphs 29–30.

[7] See Henry Kissinger, 'The End of NATO as We Know It?', *Los Angeles Times*, 15 August 1999. In December 2000, Cohen warned that NATO could become 'a relic of the past' if the Europeans opted for increased autonomy.

See William Drozdiak, 'NATO Allies Grow Edgy as Security Choices Loom', *International Herald Tribune*, 15 December 2000; and Jim Garamone, 'Cohen Says Allies Must Invest or NATO Could Become "Relic" ', *American Forces Press Service*, 5 December 2000. See also Kissinger, 'The End of NATO?'.

8   Nicole Gnesotto, 'Transatlantic Debates', *Newsletter*, WEU Institute for Security Studies, no. 29, April 2000. See also 'Excerpts from Secretary of State Madeleine Albright's Interview With the International Herald Tribune', *International Herald Tribune*, 15 January 2001. For expressions of US concern, see Charles Babington, 'A "Strong Europe" Can Depend Less On US Power, Clinton Declares', *ibid.*, 3 June 2000; and then US Ambassador to NATO Alexander Vershbow's comments in Drozdiak, 'US Seems Increasingly Uncomfortable'.

9   As argued by William Pfaff, 'NATO's Europeans Could Say "No" ', *International Herald Tribune*, 25 July 2002; see also 'If Forced To Choose, Europe Will Ditch NATO', *ibid.*, 17 August 2002. See also Klaus Becher, 'Organizing NATO for the Future', in Christina V. Balis (ed.), *Beyond the NATO Prague Summit*, CSIS Conference Report, Washington DC, September 2002, pp. 65–73.

10   See the US DoD *Quadrennial Defense Review Report*, 30 September 2001.

11   Strobe Talbott, 'Transatlantic Ties', *Newsweek*, 18 October 1999.

12   William Cohen, 'Preserving History's Greatest Alliance', *Washington Post*, 8 January 2001; 'Cohen on NATO–US–EU Partnership, Joint Defense Planning', *Washington File*, US Department of State, 6 December 2000; and the 2000 *Report on Allied Contributions to the Common Defense*.

13   *Ibid.*, p. II-2.

14   In 1997, the US Congress took it upon itself to set targets for its allies. Allies should increase the proportion of their GDP spent on defence by 10% over the previous year, or to a level commensurate with the US; they should increase military assets contributed or pledged to multinational military activities; offsets for US stationing costs should increase to 75%; foreign assistance should increase by 10% over the previous year (or to a level equal to at least 1% of GDP). *Ibid.*, p. F-1. Canada, Luxembourg, Netherlands and the UK failed to achieve these targets in all four categories. All but Greece and Turkey failed to meet the targets on defence spending, and no NATO ally met the cost-sharing target.

15   See *Strengthening Transatlantic Security – A US Strategy for the 21ˢᵗ Century*, US DoD, December 2000, part VI.

16   For a different view, see Charles Kupchan, 'In Defence of European Defence: An American Perspective', *Survival*, vol. 42, no. 2, Summer 2000.

17   Van Eekelen, *EU, WEU, and NATO*, paragraph 37.

18   Peter Schmidt, 'ESDI: Separable But Not Separate', *NATO Review*, Spring/Summer 2000.

19   Not all duplication is bad, as argued by Kori Schake, *Constructive Duplication: Reducing EU Reliance on US Military Assets*, CER Working Paper, January 2002; and 'EU Should Duplicate NATO Assets', *CER Bulletin*, Issues 18, June–July 2001.

20   Stephen Walt, 'The Ties That Fray', *The National Interest*, no. 54,

Winter 1998/1999; and Charles Grant, 'NATO's New Role', *Financial Times*, 7 August 2002.

Chapter 4

1 See Hagman, Europeiska Militära Krishanteringsförmågor, pp. 31–37.
2 Report on Allied Contributions to the Common Defense, p. III-24.
3 A conventional C-130 takes some 90 combat soldiers compared to the A400M's 120 soldiers. The C-130J-30, the extended version, takes more troops but slightly fewer cargo pallets and tons in comparison to the A400M. According to the UK, during Operation Essential Harvest in Macedonia in 2001 the C-17 took as much as four C-130 loads.
4 Haig Simonian and Ralph Atkins, 'Scharping Urges Joint Air Command', *Financial Times*, 1 November 1999.
5 The Netherlands, Norway, Denmark, Belgium and Portugal are increasing their day/night and all-weather strike capabilities, and upgrading their F-16s. This is a step in the right direction, but the upgrade is long overdue, the numbers are small and the added value is marginal. However, should the above states procure substantial numbers of PGMs such as JDAM, the increase would be significant.
6 Report on Allied Contributions to the Common Defense, p. II-2.
7 As correctly noted in Strengthening Transatlantic Security – A US Strategy for the 21st Century, US DoD, December 2000, part III.
8 Report on Allied Contributions to the Common Defense, p. II-2.
9 See Burkard Schmitt (ed.), Between Cooperation and Competition: The Transatlantic Defence Market, Chaillot Paper 44 (Paris: WEU Institute for Security Studies, January 2001).
10 See Hans Binnendijk, 'A Trans-Atlantic Division of Labor Could Undermine NATO', *International Herald Tribune*, 7 April 2001.
11 Several thousand US Marines, plus US air assets, were on call in the area should the European operation have required them. The ARFPS, later the CJPS, has experience of evacuation plans for non-NATO operations dating back to UNPROFOR and AFSOUTH OP 40104, 1992–95.
12 Annex IV Presidency Reports to the Helsinki European Council.
13 See J. P. H. Wathen, The Justification of Humanitarian Intervention Operations, unpublished paper, St. John's College, University of Cambridge, 17 July 2000.
14 The UK MoD conceded in its Kosovo after-action report that cluster bombs, because of the negative public perception, will be a less attractive alternative to precision-guided munitions and missiles such as the Maverick. Depleted-uranium armour-piercing ammunition, used by the US, will probably also fall into the same 'unsuitable' category. See Kosovo – Lessons from the Crisis, chapter 7. In humanitarian interventions and smaller-scale contingencies precision-guided munitions are a prerequisite for low collateral damage. Roberg Holzer, 'Military Trends Demand More Complex Weapons', *Defense News*, 25 October 1999.
15 Joseph Fitchett, 'Clark Recalls "Lessons" of Kosovo', *International Herald Tribune*, 3 May 2000.
16 Both the UK and France committed this capability to the EU in November 2000. France committed a capability to the

Capability Commitment Conference in November 2000 that matched this label. The EU Military Staff Intelligence Division is composed of three branches: Policy, Requirements and Production. Each member state has its own intelligence cell. The linking of national intelligence data is primarily done in the Joint Situation Centre. However, the staffing of the Intelligence Division is small, and there are no formal plans to develop it into a multi-functional and effective intelligence function.

17 The Military Staff Intelligence Division does not have civilian analysis functions or civilian leadership. It is too small and too narrowly focused, as it does not cover the whole spectrum of international assessments, conflict prevention and operational intelligence functions for EU-led operations.

18 US intelligence satellites reached 0.1m resolution in the 1980s. US-operated commercial high-resolution satellites have recently crossed the 1m resolution barrier. Helios II and the German SARLupe satellites will have resolutions of 0.8 and 0.5m respectively. 'Satellite Pictures – Private Eyes in the Sky', *The Economist*, 6 May 2000; *Charles Grant, Intimate Relations*, Centre for European Reform Working Paper, April 2000; 'European Military Satellites', *Strategic Comments*, vol. 6, no. 10, 2000; Peter de Selding, 'Three Nations Find Common Uses for Helios', *Defense News*, 13 December 1999.

19 The commercial satellite market is dominated by the US. The close links between the US government and US satellite firms mean that commercial imagery would only be available to Europeans as and when the US wants to release it (see 'European Military Satellites'). For the same reason, Europe should also look to military satellites for its communications, rather than using commercial sources. European reliance on US global-positioning systems (GPS) for sensors and weapon systems is growing. Furthermore, the US is developing precision-guided munitions for GPS-denied mode situations (i.e. GPS jamming). The US is thus free to switch off or encrypt the GPS network, either regionally or globally, albeit with consequences for trade, civil shipping and air transport. The Galileo European GPS satellite system may, in the distant future, increase European self-sufficiency, while enhancing related capabilities.

20 Naturally, any EU member state could block the CFSP/ESDP, but this would not do as much damage.

21 Helmut Schmidt, 'Don't Believe What Critics Say About the Euro', *International Herald Tribune*, 25 June 1997.

Chapter 5

1 This paper does not advocate the creation of a 'Mr ESDP' (see Daniel Keohane, 'Time for Mr ESDP', *CER Bulletin*, no. 26, October–November 2002). In practical terms, the workload of the SG/HR is a major challenge to this coordination. There would be an advantage in giving the Deputy SG a more active role. However, there are already enough cooks in the Brussels kitchen; see David Hannay, 'EU Foreign Policy: A Necessity, Not an Optional Extra', *ibid*. See also Hans-Georg Ehrhart, 'What Model for CFSP?' Chaillot Paper 55 (Paris: EU Institute for Security Studies, 2002).

[2] See Gilles Andréani, Christophe Bertram and Charles Grant, *Europe's Military Revolution*, Centre for European Reform, London, 2001.

[3] These are contacts beyond what is managed by the European Commission's Directorate-General External Relations. In mid-2002, the EU had some 140 representatives in international organisations and states. Ideally, the pillars should be able to share international points of contact. Should this not be possible, an overlapping system may be the only realistic option.

[4] Some EU candidates are concerned that EU Headline Goal demands may conflict with NATO's criteria, and thus force them to take sides. In practice, if the DCI and NATO interoperability are seen as the guiding principles, candidates' capabilities will be equally relevant for EU crisis management.

[5] Of the 2,700 employees in the General Secretariat of the Council, some 2,200 work with translations and document distribution, and only 500 focus on the various elements of the CFSP and coordination functions.

[6] For an assessment of the plans for an intelligence division in the EUMS, see Messervy-Whiting, 'The European Union's Nascent Military Staff'. As of 2001, the EUMS had established an Intelligence Division, which was composed of national representatives (and their secure communication systems) tasked with channelling national intelligence of primarily operational nature.

[7] See Becher, 'European Intelligence Policy'.

[8] Grant, *Intimate Relations*. Grant also observes that not all national intelligence services are coordinated. This adds to the challenge of funnelling national intelligence into a central EU structure.

[9] See Björn von Sydow's prescription, in 'Sweden: Swedish Minister Urges Europe To Intensify Weapons Production Co-operation', *Reuters*, 22 January 2001. It could be argued that defence industries in Europe and the US are already intertwined; see Andrew James, 'The Prospects for a Transatlantic Defense Industry', in Schmitt (ed.), *Between Cooperation and Competition*.

[10] Heisbourg, 'European Defence Takes a Leap Forward'.

[11] IISS, *The Military Balance 2002/2003*.

[12] Heisbourg, 'European Defence Takes a Leap Forward'; and François Heisbourg, 'Europe's Strategic Ambitions: The Limits of Ambiguity', *Survival*, vol. 42, no. 2, Summer 2000. See also the recommendations in Andréani, Bertram and Grant, *Europe's Military Revolution*.

[13] See Tim Garden and John Roper, *Pooling Forces*, Centre for European Reform, December 1999, www.cer.org.uk.

[14] See Klaus Naumann, *Europe's Military Ambitions*, Centre for European Reform, June–July 2000, www.cer.org.uk.

[15] Preferably, there should be a correlation between EU and NATO rapid-reaction forces for interoperability reasons – whatever the institutional banner for an operation.

[16] See 'Communication from the Commission to the Council and the European Parliament "Towards integrated management of the external borders of the Member States of the European Union" ', Secretary-General of the

European Commission to Javier Solana, 12 May 2002 (9139/02).

[17] The current division of labour between the Director-General for external affairs (more specifically DGE VIII), which has responsibility for police operations, and the Military Staff, focused on operational military crisis management, is not satisfactory.

[18] Much institutional coordination depends on such banal factors as the cooperative nature of individuals in the two organisations, competence and time.

[19] For suggestions as to how to develop an EU White Paper, see Heisbourg, 'Europe's Strategic Ambitions'. See also John Vinocur, 'EU Defense Autonomy Lacks a Unifying Voice', *International Herald Tribune*, 9 April 2001.

[20] Nicole Gnesotto and Karl Kaiser, 'European–American Interaction', in Heisbourg (ed.), *European Defence: Making It Work*.

[21] In January 2001, it was decided that the Political and Security Committee and the NAC would meet at least three times during each EU presidency. Formally, the first PSC–NAC meeting was held on 5 February 2001. Extra *ad hoc* meetings are also arranged to discuss operational matters. The first GAC–NAC meeting was held in Budapest on 30 May 2001.

[22] The experience of the Euro-Atlantic Partnership Council, OSCE and UN, although different in scale and scope, may indicate that the main function of a joint forum is dialogue and confidence-building, rather than far reaching cooperation and decision-shaping.